THE SEE JOURNEY

YOUR EMERGING IDENTITY

WHAT PEOPLE ARE SAYING

"I have become aware of recognizing I don't have to live in a negative state, but I can release it in the exchange for something greater. You and Mark have been used in my life as a breath of fresh air... I sincerely mean that. Your work is opening up doors to change lives forever..."
- D.C., Vacaville, California

"As a teen I spent most of it crying due to emotional conflict. Now I have a way of releasing it. With no drugs, I am physically healthier and a lot happier on the inside." - S.N., Texas

"Such quick and effective tools for forgiveness of deep hurts from the past. I just have to think back to the little drawing and I feel relief. I know the true desires that I have for that one. Also they are truly free and so am I. It's so happy! The thought can't come back." - California

"Thank you so much for this life skill that I will continue to use frequently."
- A.R., California

"I took my second EQ test and I went from 87% to 96%! I think you are on to something!!" - California

"I enjoyed the SEE program. It was very beneficial for me. The tools I gained are a part of my life and a guidance for future challenging situations. The experience of drawing a positive situation change was very empowering and freeing for me. I was able to put this new energy into dance and music and rejuvenate my creative flow." - Chris S., Pendleton, OR

"My identity was revealed through this program and I felt great after each session! I love SEE and know it will make a significant impact on people's mental, emotional and spiritual wellbeing!"
- Gabrielle B. Las Vegas, Nevada

"I am thrilled about the SEE program and I am excited to see how it will help others. People often brush off creativity as just a form of entertainment, but I strongly believe in the power of the creative arts and the ways they express the very depths of our humanity." - Vincent M., Las Vegas, Nevada

"Before SEE, I was not able to connect the dots between my thoughts, emotions and my behavior. I wasn't able to explain why I felt what I felt, why I thought what I thought and why I responded the way I responded to things. Now it seems as if my brain and my emotions have connected, and I have better performance in my day to day life. I feel more free and I have more clarity than I have ever had before. I highly recommend it to every living person on this earth." - Carynn C., Las Vegas, Nevada

"SEE has helped me have a beautiful way to exchange my negative emotions into positive emotions, to calm and center myself. I love SEE. It has helped me expand my knowledge and feel better about myself."
- Kimberly R., Las Vegas, Nevada

"For most of my life I have struggle with expressing myself emotionally. I believe this has affected a lot of my relationships because it was difficult for me to be emotionally intimate and vulnerable with people. It was hard for me at times to communicate my feelings to my husband because I had a hard time identifying why I was feeling a certain way and I would get frustrated. Since doing SEE, I have been noticing a difference in the way I handle and communicate my emotions. If I am feeling upset or angry for no apparent reason, I can get to the bottom of why I'm feeling that way more quickly by being more aware of my emotions and doing a SEE drawing, if I have to. I am finding that I get into negative moods less often, and when I do it is easier for me to get out of them. I believe this has helped my relationship with my husband and has helped me to grow and mature emotionally."
- Las Vegas, Nevada

"I believe that the SEE program helped me to recognize my feelings in times when normally I would not know how I felt or would deny my feelings. I learned that its OK to feel that my feelings are valid. I've learned how to turn negative feelings around not just with words but by allowing myself to feel positivity. I also learned to find the value in art and how to displace emotions in my own art." - Ashley B., Las Vegas, Nevada

THE SEE JOURNEY

YOUR EMERGING IDENTITY

MICHELLE KAMRATH

Copyright © 2021 by Michelle Kamrath

Corrales, New Mexico

For more information go to:

MKArtAcademy.com

These methods and processes contained in this book
are the intellectual property of Michelle Kamrath.

This book is protected by the
copyright laws of the United States of America.
This book may not be copied or reprinted for commercial use.
All rights reserved.

Printed in the U.S.A.

THE SEE JOURNEY: YOUR EMERGING IDENTITY

Version 1

ISBN-13: 978-1-7330368-4-9

CONTENTS

INTRODUCTION — 9

LEVEL 1 PERSONAL AWARENESS — 15

- DISCOVERY 1: LEARN THE BASICS — 17
- DISCOVERY 2: SEE YOUR VALUE — 25
- DISCOVERY 3: EXPLORE YOUR IDENTITY — 32
- DISCOVERY 4: FIND YOUR PURPOSE — 39
- DISCOVERY 5: UNWRAP YOUR GIFTS — 45
- DISCOVERY 6: BE YOUR OWN BEST FRIEND — 51

LEVEL 2 BUILD RELATIONSHIPS — 57

- DISCOVERY 7: LETTING IT GO — 59
- DISCOVERY 8: DRAW THE LINE — 65
- DISCOVERY 9: CHOOSE LOVE — 71

LEVEL 3 STAY EMPOWERED — 79

- DISCOVERY 10: ENCOURAGE YOURSELF — 81

DRAWING JOURNAL — 87

THE LANGUAGE OF THE LINE — 149

FURTHER STUDY — 161

WORKS CITED — 173

THE SEE JOURNEY
INTRODUCTION

This book is the result of a ten-year journey of discovery for me and my husband, Mark. It came through some desperation and some inspiration, but it has changed our lives forever. The SEE Journey teaches a creative technique that allows us to gain new perspectives about who we are and where we are going. It changes our focus and engages our creative visual minds so we can graphically see what is true about us. It does not say, "stop doing that," but rather it says, "see this instead." If we can see it, we can become it.

Our SEE journey began after 30 years of marriage, two amazing children, and many beautiful memories, but in the last ten years, Mark seemed less able to handle stressful situations, and I didn't know why. Living in the congested Bay Area in California seemed to only make it worse. Traffic jams were the biggest challenge, and there were many times while driving, Mark would call me in a panic behind a line of stopped cars on the freeway. I would calm him down, urge him to exit until it cleared. I even thought if we moved to a remote area, it might eliminate this problem. Waiting in line at a drive-thru was almost an impossibility for him. He experienced anxiety, and had to get out of the car, while I paid for our food. It caused arguments and miscommunication, and with each passing year, it got worse. We were frustrated and had no clear path forward.

We sought counseling and worked through a year program together. It helped us but did not address the emotional issues Mark was still having. He could not tell what he was feeling at any given moment. I was grateful for the counseling, advice, and progress we made, but I was not ready to give up. I decided to research everything I could find on emotional intelligence and how to increase it. First, I had Mark take an online Emotional Intelligence Test. It gave him a baseline before we started. His low score on the test (102 out of 155) reflected his inability to identity his feelings. He scored in the 58th percentile out of 100.

The first book I read was *Emotional Intelligence* written by Daniel Goleman. Emotional intelligence (EQ) is the skill to recognize and identify emotions and then talk about them and eventually manage them. If we do not recognize our emotions, we have little chance of managing them. Goleman explained that people may have a high intelligence academically and yet lack the intelligence needed emotionally in relationships. They cannot pick up on facial clues and body gestures so they do not know how others are feeling. Goleman explained that, "...social intelligence...is the key part of what makes people do well in the workplace and in the practicalities of life" (42). These two intelligences are derived from two different minds, one emotional and one rational.

Goleman explained, "...these abilities [of emotional intelligence] can preserve our most prized relationships, or their lack corrode them." Furthermore, the lack of emotional intelligence in marriage can cause "emotional rifts that eventually can tear their relationship apart" (133). In a study run by John Gottman, a University of Washington psychologist, Gottman predicted with 94 percent accuracy which couples would divorce within three years, just by analyzing hours of the emotional currents in their conversations (Goleman, 134). From personal experience, I knew these frustrations well. It wears both people down, communication is weak, and feelings consistently get hurt.

> **EMOTIONAL INTELLIGENCE:**
> - Knowing One's Emotions
> - Managing Emotions
> - Motivating Oneself
> - Knowing Other's Emotions
> - Handling Relationships

Another book *Emotional Intelligence 2.0*, written by Travis Bradberry and Jean Greaves, states, "The communication between your emotional and rational 'brains' is the physical source of emotional intelligence" (Bradberry, 7). They state: "Only 36% of the people tested are able to accurately identify their emotions as they happen" (Bradberry, 13). So, Mark was not alone. Sixty-four percent of those tested did not know what they were feeling, when they were feeling it. This shows a breakdown in communication between the emotional and rational minds in most people tested. They, of course, had emotions, but they were unaware of what they were. Goleman writes:

> "...self-awareness would seem to require an activated neocortex, particularly the language areas, attuned to identify and name the emotions being aroused" (47). ...though the circuits of the emotional brain may react with feelings, the neocortex is not able to sort out these feelings

> **WE HAVE TWO MINDS:**
> - Rational
> - Emotional

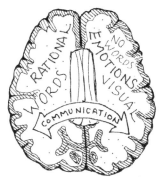

A cross-section of the brain looking down on the right and left hemisphere. Generally, words are processed in one hemisphere and emotions in the other.

and add the nuance of language to them…if you could put words to what you felt, it was yours…having no words for feelings means not making the feelings your own" (52).

The communication between the emotional and the rational minds seemed to play an essential role in emotional intelligence. This seemed to be the root of Mark's trouble. He could not verbalize what he was feeling, or even *if* he was feeling anything. It was as if his rational mind could not access what his emotional mind was feeling, so it remained a mystery to him. This was starting to make sense why Mark had such difficulty in handling stressful situations.

Goleman writes about people who are in recovery from trauma (post-traumatic stress disorder or PTSD). In therapy, they are encouraged to give a complete retelling of the traumatic event. For example, children who were subject to trauma would instinctively play out the trauma as games, retelling the event repeatedly. In this way, the children connect their emotional feelings with words,

> Communication between our two minds is the source of emotional intelligence.

making communication pathways between their two minds, so that they could deal with the trauma easier.

Goleman also sites research that shows how parents play an important role in teaching their children to be aware of their emotions through dialog. For example, research shows that parents modified their children's "fight or flight" instinct "by coaching them emotionally: talking to children about their feelings and how to understand them…" (Goleman, 227).

This reoccurring theme kept surfacing. Emotional intelligence was a result of our two minds communicating with one another. Once I realized this, bells started going off in my head! I am a professional artist and have taught art for over 20 years. I immediately thought of an art book I read years ago by Betty Edwards titled, *Drawing on the Artist Within*. She wrote about an exercise she developed that helped her art students increase creativity.

> "Ordinary words cannot express the complex language of our feelings. Our goal is to dredge up that inner life of the mind by using an alternative visual language to

give it tangible form--in short, to make inner thought visible" (Edwards 66).

In Edwards' exercise, a student drew what he felt and then labelled his drawing with words. This way the emotional drawings were combined with the rational words. This sounded like the two minds were communicating, which is the key to increasing emotional intelligence! So, I decide this was what Mark needed! "We are going to draw!" He was reluctant at first, but slowly, with much coaxing, he learned how to draw his emotions and give words to the marks on his page.

Mark continued doing simple line drawings (16 total) over the next nine months and took his second EQ test. The test results were amazing! His EQ score increased 21 points, from 102 to 123. This time he scored in the 95th percentile! We were shocked at the difference this simple creative act had made in his score. We also started noticing that some of his anxiety was beginning to subside.

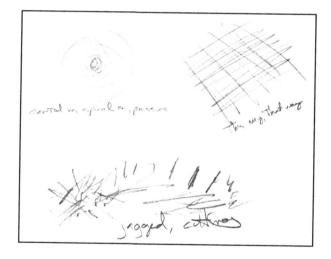

In August 2012, around two o'clock in the morning, Mark woke up filled with anxiety. I was sound asleep. He got out of bed and headed down to the living room to shake off the feelings. Usually, these feelings lasted a few hours and when he was too tired to care anymore, he would crawl back into bed and go back to sleep.

As Mark headed downstairs, his stomach knotted up with tension as usual, but this time he heard my voice in his head saying, "Just draw it." Out of frustration, he grabbed some paper and a pencil and began to draw out the feelings that raged inside. These emotions intensely flowed out as three drawings.

He labelled the first one "carried in, spiral, pressure." The second was labelled, "this way, that way," and the third, "jagged, cutting." There it was. His emotional state stared back at him from the paper. He finally could see what had kept him up so many nights. He thought to

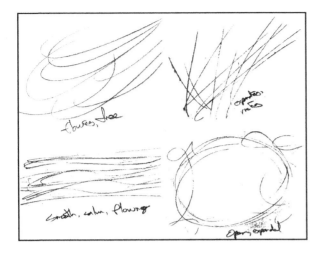

himself, "Now what?"

Then, the most amazing thing happened. He got another thought, "What do you want to feel like?" "What?" He asked himself. The question came to him again, "What do you want to feel like?" This was a spark of insight! Mark took another piece of paper and quickly drew four new drawings to express what he wanted to feel.

He finished the drawings and labelled them "flowing, free, smooth, calm, flowing, expanding, rising, open and expanded." Then, in the stillness of the night, he thought, "Now flag it." He turned and found two small flags and with a flag in each hand, he traced out each drawing in the air. In a matter of moments, the negative, constricting feelings gave way to the flowing flags. Positive new feelings of peace, freedom, and openness flooded in to replace the anxiety.

After he finished flagging each drawing a few times, he stopped and realized he was able to turn his anxiety around. These feelings that normally kept him up many hours, were completely gone. He returned to bed and went back to sleep. In the morning, he told me what had happened. Right then, we felt this was a special gift to a weary soul. Mark coined this three-step process as Strategic Emotional Exchange and SEE was born. Over the next seven months, six or seven times he woke up with similar anxious thoughts. He repeated the same SEE process, and each time felt calmer and was able to go back to sleep.

On one Thursday in April, Mark had to drive the car into San Francisco for work because rain was in the forecast. On dry days, he rode his motorcycle, so he could easily maneuver around stopped traffic. However, this day the freeways were sure to be backed up, when a one-hour trip takes two and a half to get home. But, unlike so many times when stopped traffic and the feeling of being trapped would cause Mark to panic, this drive was different. Instead of feeling anxious, he felt relaxed. He told me it felt like he was rowing a boat through the water, as the windshield wipers kept rhythm in the slow-moving stream of cars. He did not *make* himself feel calm. He just was.

He had been in a situation that normally would have overwhelmed him but instead, his mind shifted into a peaceful mode. His response was not fear or anxiety, but relaxation and tranquility. Through many months of using the SEE technique, he consistently exchanged anxiety for peacefulness. Did SEE retrain his brain to respond differently? After another six months of doing SEE regularly, Mark's EQ score went up another 6 points (129 out of 155), which put him in the 97th percentile!

I began teaching SEE to friends and family with the hope that they would experience similar results. Many people had breakthroughs and gained insights. Also, I learned a great deal and began to see consistent themes emerge in the drawings. Low self-image and limiting beliefs consistently resurfaced in the negative drawings, which expressed feelings of worthlessness, stupidity, and incompetence. These feelings attacked a person's God-given value, identity, purpose, and ability. After coaching over 50 people through the SEE process, I have compiled what I have learned into this workbook and want to take you on the same journey! I want to teach you this tool called SEE, so you may find insights into your inner thoughts and feelings and see yourself and others, through the lens of compassion and empathy. May you exchange any limiting beliefs holding you back, increase your emotional intelligence, better manage your feelings, and believe the powerful truths that will move you towards your best life.

LEVEL 1
PERSONAL AWARENESS

*"Until you make the unconscious conscious,
it will direct your life and you will call it fate."*
— *Carl Jung*

THE SEE JOURNEY
DISCOVERY 1
LEARN THE BASICS

Before you start on your own SEE journey, we suggest you take an Emotional Intelligence test to give yourself a baseline. You can find the test online at Queendom.com. Search the site for "Emotional Intelligence Test."

Record your score or print off your results and keep them safe, so you can retest after doing SEE for a few months. This is a concrete way to see your progress and improvement.

In this section, we will learn the basics of how to draw our feelings. Then, by labeling our drawings with words, we will open up communication between our verbal and visual minds. This will help us recognize our feelings and will naturally increase our emotional awareness and intelligence.

First, let's learn about lines and the information they provide. Using a pencil, draw a line about three inches long, as fast as possible in the blank space below.

Draw in this space:

Now, beside that line, draw another line. Try to copy the first one as best as you can, only this time, draw it as slowly as possible. After you have done that, look at your two lines.

If you have never seen these before, would you be able to tell which one was drawn fast? Why is that? What about the first line indicates it was drawn fast? Betty Edwards explains the aspect of speed and time in a line.

> "Thus, time itself is recorded in its weight, its roughness or smoothness. Thus time itself is recorded in drawings—not in the linear, measured way...but in the way time

is recorded in a human face, for example. Time becomes an embedded quality, which can be seen and comprehended" (Edwards 61).

Now, look at your lines again. Which line looks more confident? Which one looks insecure and timid? A line can express these nuances of feeling just by its quality and visual properties. Fast, smooth lines convey one feeling, while slow, shaky lines convey another. Betty Edwards sums it up:

> "Thus, every line is a statement, a form of communication between the individual who made the line and the individual who views it. A drawing is a far more complex mode of expression, revealing of a wide range of thoughts and emotion, many of which originate in a realm beyond conscious awareness. We can 'read' a line. Can we 'read' a drawing? If so, perhaps we can take a step in the direction of gaining access to that part of the mind which knows…more than it knows it knows—the same part of the brain that asks the beautiful question, ponders the unsolved problem, takes the initial step in the creative process…" (Edwards 65).

There is more to our simple lines than we thought! I am going to lead you through an exercise that will teach you the first step of the SEE Exchange. You will begin to learn how a simple line can communicate time, feelings and those mysterious things that our emotional minds know.

D1 EXERCISE
YOUR VISUAL DICTIONARY

Before you are able to start using the SEE method, you will need to learn the basic skill of drawing your feelings. It is not hard, but it takes some practice getting comfortable with and being okay with scribbling as an expression. Your drawings will not be anything other than lines, dots, scratch marks, and doodles. They will not be drawings of things, like a cat or a house. Instead, they will be abstract expressions of what a feeling looks like as a drawing. No two people will draw the same thing for each feeling, because we all process and express our experiences differently. Your visual dictionary will be unique to you and help you interpret future drawings when problem-solving.

INSTRUCTIONS

You will need a pencil and eraser.

 Write today's date at the top. Then, read the word under the box and remember a time when you felt it. Picture the situation like a silent movie. Put yourself there and allow yourself to feel it fully. Picture the location and who is there. Do not hear what they are saying, but watch the action like a silent movie, if you can. See facial expressions and body language.

 Once you picture the situation and feel it, hold onto that feeling and then go from that feeling into the first box with your pencil and allow your self to draw what it feels like.

A FEW DRAWING GUIDELINES

- Don't pre-think. Try not to plan out ahead of time what you are going to draw. Try to feel it and then draw organically from that feeling.

- Don't draw pictures. Allow yourself the freedom to scribble, as you express each feeling. Don't draw actual objects or symbol shapes, like hearts or stars. We want to draw the basic, rudimentary line.

- You may erase. Keep going until it feels complete. Erase anything that doesn't feel right. You cannot do this wrong. It is right if it feels right to you.

- Don't judge. You are practicing to make your inner feelings visible. This is probably new to you, so don't judge your marks in any way. Rather, give yourself the freedom and permission to express your feelings using this new visual vocabulary.

 Do all 16 boxes. Begin by reading each emotion, picturing it, feeling it and then draw the feeling. If you encounter one that you have difficulty with, pass and go on to the next one. Do as many as you can while remembering the guidelines above.

 Look at each drawing and write down any words that come to mind. There is no "right" answer. If it looks dark, write "dark." If it looks like a mountain, then write, "mountain." This exercise will help you identify hidden feelings by giving you a vocabulary for them. To better understand line drawings and how they communicate feelings, refer to the section, "The Language of the Line" in the back.

D1 EXERCISE
YOUR VISUAL DICTIONARY

DATE:

ANGER

INSPIRATION

LOVE

PEACE

DEPRESSION

CONFUSION

JOY

THANKFUL

WORRY	GENEROUS
FREE	INSULTED
DISGUSTED	EXCITED
GUILTY	CURIOUS

D1 HOMEWORK THIS WEEK

1. Add words to your drawings. Look back at each one of your drawings and ask yourself what do they look like. Write down any other words that come to mind when you look at each one, on the lines next to each drawing. If it looks dark, write "dark." This will help by increasing your vocabulary for your feelings. Check off this assignment this week, once you have finished it.

☐ I finished it! Date

2. What similarities do you see? Look at this next section and compare your drawings of anger, love, depression, joy, inspiration, peace, confusion, and thankfulness to the examples given and circle any that are similar to yours.

☐ I finished it! Date

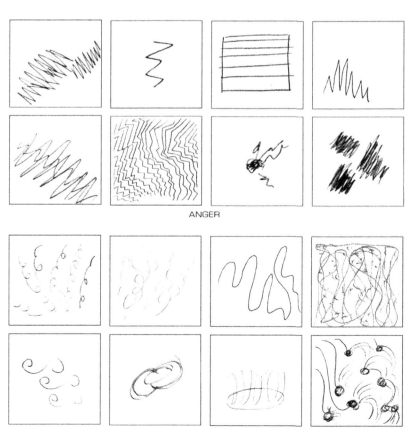

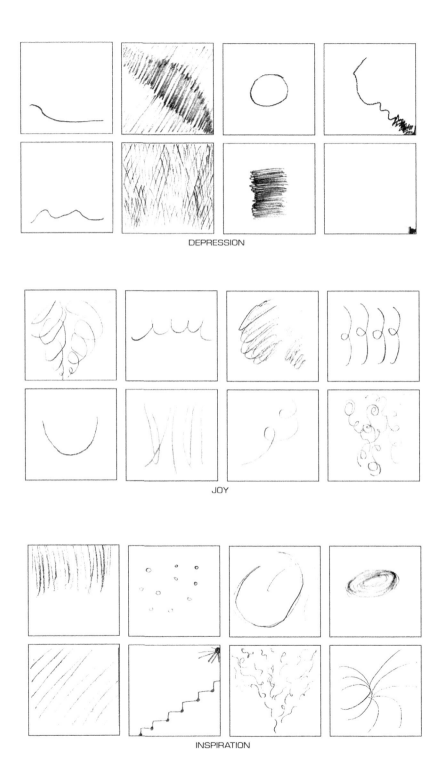

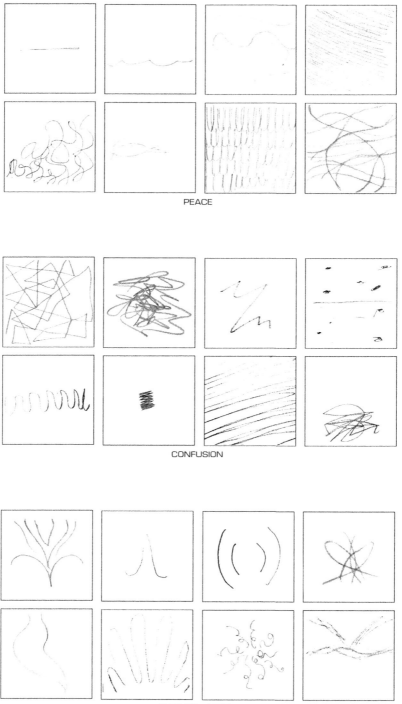

DISCOVERY TWO   25

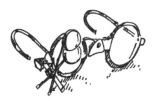

THE SEE JOURNEY
DISCOVERY 2
SEE YOUR VALUE

In Discovery One you learned how to draw 16 basic feelings. This fundamental exercise has given you visual pictures of the invisible. It may have been awkward and new for you, but as we progress, you will become more comfortable with this process and doubt yourself less.

Our journey begins with the most powerful force in the world: love. It has the power to change things. Nelson Mandela writes in Long Walk to Freedom, "People must learn to hate, and if they can learn to hate, they can be taught to love, for love comes more naturally to the human heart than its opposite..." (622). I believe SEE teaches us how to love ourselves at a deep level so any thoughts of self-doubt can be exchanged and replaced. Self-doubt questions a person's value, identity, purpose, and ability. I believe there are four universal truths that speak to these: everyone is priceless, everyone has a unique identity, everyone has a purpose, and everyone has gifts and talents that support each purpose.

UNIVERSAL TRUTH 1
EVERY PERSON IS PRICELESS

UNIVERSAL TRUTH 2
EVERY PERSON HAS A UNIQUE IDENTITY

UNIVERSAL TRUTH 3
EVERY PERSON HAS A PURPOSE IN LIFE

UNIVERSAL TRUTH 4
EVERY PERSON HAS GIFTS AND TALENTS

You may or may not believe these about yourself or others yet, and that's okay. We all have been raised in a world that does not teach these, but that doesn't make them untrue. Let's look at the first universal truth.

UNIVERSAL TRUTH 1
EVERY PERSON IS PRICELESS

> The first universal truth teaches that each person's value is priceless and is present at birth and remains constant a lifetime. A person's value does not come from this world, so nothing a person does in this world can add to or subtract from that value. Each person counts for one, which makes no one person worth more or less than any other person and no one is here for the sole purpose of another.

All people everywhere are valuable and priceless, and yet many believe lies about themselves that contradict this truth.

Truth:
"I am priceless."

Lies:
"I'm worthless."
"I'm a loser."
"I'm a waste of other people's time."
"I don't deserve to be here."
"My value is determined by my job, education, accomplishments, reputation, or net worth."

These lies can come from our past experiences and build a false identity of who we are and how we fit into this world. Many of these lies go back to our childhood to things we were told. They eat away at our self-confidence and stop us from acting, speaking, and being the person of value that we already are. Instead, they become part of a false narrative when we accept them.

These lies might surface at times when we call ourselves names, or they might inhabit our living spaces when they fill us with self-hate. Fear builds on top of these lies as we believe them. Then, because we believe them, they may become a reality even though they are based on false assumptions. I might believe I am stupid, and so I do something stupid. This negative experience reinforces to me that what I believe is true. When experiences reinforce these lies we

believe, they are like bricks. One experience is built upon another, all making up a wall that stands between us and the life we want to live. SEE aims to eliminate the lies and the fear they bring so we can dismantle this wall and move forward into those things waiting for us.

There are two driving forces in life: love and fear. One of these will be at the root of our thoughts and actions. Our positive feelings come from love and the truths we believe about ourselves and others. Likewise, our negative feelings stem from fear and the lies we believe. These are powerful motivators and dictate how we will perceive ourselves and life situations. When we refuse to fear and choose to love instead, we open the door to positive changes.

CORE CONCEPT 1: PEOPLE ARE MOTIVATED BY LOVE OR FEAR

- All thoughts, behaviors, and actions come out of love or fear.
- Love and fear each have their own cycle which flow opposite one another, and each promotes more of the same.
- Love is stronger than fear.

This dominant force of love has the power to eliminate fear. Love can dispel fear, just as light can eliminate darkness. The darkness has no power in itself because it has no substance. When the light is introduced, the darkness has to go. Light does not have to wrangle the darkness to the floor, it simply takes its place, because darkness is the absence of light. Love and goodness are always stronger than fear and darkness, because they exist only in the absence of love.

CORE CONCEPT 2: LOVE YOURSELF, SO YOU CAN LOVE OTHERS

If you hate yourself, you will find it next to impossible to love another. If you criticize yourself, you will find it easy to criticize others. How you treat yourself will be a reflection of how you think of and treat others. Love yourself, then you can extend honor and love to others.

Denying or judging our negative feelings does little to help. The feelings just go underground, only to surface when we don't want them. This exercise will help us process the negative attitudes we have about ourselves and exchange them for empowered states of mind. Today's exercise will help us process limiting beliefs we have about ourselves, so we can exchange them for what is true and move beyond them into confidence and love.

D2 EXERCISE
VISUALIZE SELF-CONFIDENCE

In this exercise, we will be exchanging the feeling of being marginalized, less than, and pushed aside for the feeling of being valued, confident, and worthwhile.

 DRAW YOUR FEELING

REMEMBER A TIME: Remember a time you felt insecure or worthless. Try to think of a specific time, rather than just a general feeling.

WRITE THE DATE AND THE SITUATION: Once you have decided on a specific situation, go to the next formatted page and write today's date on the line at the top right side. Also, write down briefly what situation you are remembering for this exercise.

PICTURE IT: Put yourself in the situation and allow yourself to feel it fully. Picture the location and who is there. Do not hear what they are saying, but watch the action like a silent movie. See facial expressions and body language.

DRAW IT: Once you feel it, hold that feeling and allow it to flow out of you and into the box labelled 1. Draw it as you feel it. Remember try not to pre-think what it *should* look like. Don't draw any symbol shapes. You may erase. Don't judge your marks. It is right if it feels right to you.

GIVE IT WORDS: After you have drawn it, ask yourself what words come to mind when you look at it, and then label it with as many words as you can. Give it a title by asking, "What word or phrase would describe this drawing?" Write the title on the line under the drawing.

 DRAW WHAT YOU *WANT* TO FEEL

ASK THIS QUESTION: We know what that negative feeling looks like now and we even have words that describe it. Now ask yourself, "What do I *want* to feel?" Instead of feeling this first drawing, what would you rather feel?

FEEL IT: Allow yourself the time to feel this new feeling. It may take some imagination, but allow yourself the freedom to feel what you *want* to feel.

DRAW IT: Once you feel it, hold that feeling and allow it to come out in the box labelled 2.

GIVE IT WORDS: Now, ask yourself, "What words come to mind when I look at it?" Now, label it with as many words that you can think of. Give it a title by asking, "What word or phrase would describe this drawing?" Write the title on the title line under the drawing. This is your first *power image*.

 WHAT ARE THE LIES?

The truth is you are priceless! No amount of money could buy you! So, you may have feelings that are based on lies you believe about yourself. What lies could you be believing about yourself that caused the feelings in the first drawing? Write down these lies on the lines provided. Now, write "LIES" over the top of them.

 WHAT IS THE TRUTH?

What is true about you that is represented in the second drawing? It may help to use the words you wrote next to the drawing to define the truth. Try to write it as an affirmative sentence. For example, "I am …"

 HEAD, HEART & HANDS

 Science knows that we learn through the movement of our bodies. To exchange the unwanted feeling of insecurity for the positive feeling of confidence, draw your second drawing in the air with your arm in front of you. As you do, feel the positive feelings and repeat the title out loud. These three actions connect your head, heart and hands. You are agreeing with this new empowered state on three levels: your verbal mind, your visual mind, and your physical body.

 REFLECTIONS & INSIGHTS

Reflect on the impact of this exercise and write down any insights you may have on the next page.

EXERCISE
VISUALIZE SELF-CONFIDENCE

DATE: SITUATION:

Think of a time you felt insecure or worthless. Allow yourself to see the situation, but hear no sound. Allow yourself to feel it and from that feeling, express it with lines in the first box below. Don't draw symbols and you may erase if you like. It's right, if it feels right to you.

1. DRAW YOUR FEELING
Draw the feeling of insecurity in the box, label it with words, and give it a title on the lines below.

TITLE

2. DRAW WHAT YOU *WANT* TO FEEL
*Draw what you **want** to feel in the box, label it with words, and give it a title on the lines below.*

TITLE

3 WHAT ARE THE LIES?

What lies could you be believing about yourself that caused the feelings in the first drawing? Write these lies below. After you write them, cross them out and write "LIES" over them.

4 WHAT IS THE TRUTH?

What is true about you that is represented in the second drawing? It may help to use the words you wrote next to the drawing to define the truth. Try to write it as an affirmative sentence.

5 HEAD, HEART & HANDS

Trace your new drawing in the air with your hand and arm. Say the title and feel the feeling as you do this. Picture the air around you changing to a positive atmosphere as you draw this new image in front of you.

6 REFLECTIONS & INSIGHTS

We call this second drawing a "Power Image." This is an image that can empower you if you get hit with the feeling of worthlessness. You simply retrace your image in the air with your arm and feel the freedom of what is true. How do you feel after drawing your new image in the air?

D2 HOMEWORK THIS WEEK

Redraw your power image for this week in the box below and write your truth statement on the lines below. Then, at least once a day this week, simply retrace your power image in the air with your arm and feel the freedom of what is true. Say the title out loud or the words association with this new image. You are training yourself to think differently. You are exchanging any current feeling of insecurity with the feelings based on what is true about you. Instead of the limiting thoughts dictating your attitude and actions, you are forging new pathways of thought that better align with your true identity and purpose. Check off your completion each day below.

1. **Redraw your power image in the box from this week's exercise and write its title.**

2. **Write the truth about yourself as an "I am" statement.**

_____
_____
_____

Title

3. **Draw your power image in the air once a day this week, while repeating the truth out loud. Check it off each day.**

Day 1 ☐ I finished! Date _____
Day 2 ☐ I finished! Date _____
Day 3 ☐ I finished! Date _____
Day 4 ☐ I finished! Date _____
Day 5 ☐ I finished! Date _____
Day 6 ☐ I finished! Date _____

TRUTH
"I am priceless, a person of immeasurable worth."

THE SEE JOURNEY
DISCOVERY 3
EXPLORE YOUR IDENTITY

What we believe about our identity is always at the root of our victories and our failures. So much of what we believe about ourselves has come from what other people have told us. Children look to those around them to teach them who they are and how they fit into this world. In school, we look to other kids to give us our place in the pecking order of our peers. We become influenced by what is said to us and about us. Most often, we accept it as the truth and begin living it as our identity.

UNIVERSAL TRUTH 2
EVERY PERSON HAS A UNIQUE IDENTITY

> This identity resides in the spirit of a person. It is that part of each of us that gives each person importance and significance, and no two identities are exactly alike. Like a person's fingerprint, so is the imprint of the soul. Therefore, no one can replace any other and the impact each life makes here on earth. Each is born with a purpose, and each has gifts and talents that contribute to the well-being of each other. Each has dreams, desires, and aspirations that are loving, kind, compassionate, creative, courageous, bold, unwavering, strong, and valiant. They are protective, nurturing, supporting, caring, unyielding, uncompromising, willing to sacrifice self, willing to give of self, and willing to bring help to the suffering. These are the parts of the human spirit that make up the identities of every one.

"Sticks and stones may break my bones, but names can never hurt me," is a saying we have all heard, but it is not true. Labels and names can define our identity more than we know. SEE allows us to exchange the negative words for what is true. Lies about your identity might sound like, "I am a nobody," "My life is a mistake," or "I will never amount to anything."

We can look at our current situation and think this defines us and who we are, but what if it doesn't?

No two people are exactly alike. Even twins have unique fingerprints. So, we all have individual identities and what we bring to the world, and yet we all have the same value: priceless. In society, some people are perceived as more valuable than others, and that those with less value should be just like those with greater value. I believe it is just the opposite; we all have the same value, but with completely different identities.

Your personality is linked with your identity and it brings your passion for your space in this world. It brings conviction and is what drives you. It is wrapped around things you love to do that come easily for you. It can be developed from things you have overcome, and it might bring solutions to others. You might be a leader, a supporter, an influencer, or a visionary. There is usually a cluster of attributes that define you and your strengths.

One concept to understand concerning your identity is knowing that when you overextend yourself in your strengths, they can work against you and become a weakness.

> **CORE CONCEPT 3:** A STRENGTH CAN BECOME A WEAKNESS
>
> Your personality is linked with your identity. Your identity brings passion for your space in this world. It brings conviction and is what drives you, but when you overextend a strength, it can work against you and become a weakness.

For instance, someone may be a leader, but if they overextend their gifting, they may just end up being bossy. What comes naturally for them goes beyond too far, and it just ends up irritating others. Someone else may be very good at supporting others, but when overextended, their strength begins to care too much about what others think, and they become people-pleasers. The key to your unique identity is learning to balance those things you are good at so you don't overextend them. Many times, our balance is off because of some fear we have not eliminated yet. The leader may be afraid others will not follow, so they will resort to telling others what to do, rather than just taking the lead and allowing others to follow.

> **CORE CONCEPT 4:** FACTS DON'T DEFINE YOU
>
> We might believe a lie about ourselves and then act according to that lie. Our actions become the "facts" in our lives. These facts reinforce a false identity, even though they are based on lies. So, we can't look at past actions or circumstances in our lives and define ourselves according to those. If they were based on lies, then they are not reliable to give us our true identity.

Identity statements always begin with two words: "I am..." I am fat. I am dumb. I am a loser. I am no good. Every time we confess statements that do not line up with the universal truth of identity, we agree with lies. These judgments may be so common we don't even realize we make them. You might argue that you are fat, according to the weight charts published by the government, but being fat is a fact, not a truth. The difference is huge! A fact can change, but the truth will never change. You might be fat today, but then go on a diet and start an exercise program. You might lose the extra weight and become a professional body builder! It has happened. The fact changed about your weight, but that did not change the truth about your identity and your value. We can't base our identity on facts. We will always be priceless, regardless of our weight. Our value and identity do not come from the facts in our lives; they come from what is true about us.

D3 EXERCISE
EXCHANGE A FALSE IDENTITY

In this exercise, we will explore those words spoken to you about your identity and exchange them for images and words that are true. Just because someone said something, it does not make it true. Remember, people carry their own garbage and like to spew it onto others. Take this time to exchange any negatives that have been thrown your way and move closer to who you are.

> Here are some prompts you can use for this exercise. Choose the one that most resonates with you.
>
> **Called Names:** What have people told you or said about you? Were you ever bullied or made to feel stupid or insignificant? Have people called you names? Do you ever call yourself names? If so, what do you say? Has someone else ever said that? Who has said it? Who else? Picture a situation where you were made fun of, bullied, or called names. Feel what that felt like, hold onto it and draw it in the first box in Discovery 3 in the Drawing Journal section.
>
> **Repeated Patterns:** A false identity comes from a place deep inside of us. This identity can surface over and over as a repeated response. Is there something that repeats in your life that stops you from being confident? Picture one time when this pattern came up.

Once you choose your prompt, go to the next page and follow the instructions to exchange the feeling of a false identity.

# EXERCISE
EXCHANGE A FALSE IDENTITY

DATE: _____ SITUATION: _____

Think of a time you were called names or have experienced negative repeated patterns in your life. Allow yourself to see the situation, but hear no sound. Allow yourself to feel it and from that feeling, express it with lines in the first box below. Don't draw symbols and you may erase if you like. It's right if it feels right to you.

1. DRAW THE FEELING

Draw the feeling in the box, label it with words, and give it a title on the lines below.

TITLE _____

2. DRAW WHAT YOU *WANT* TO FEEL

*Draw what you **want** to feel in the box, label it with words, and give it a title on the lines below.*

3. WHAT ARE THE LIES?

What lies could you be believing about yourself that caused the feelings in the first drawing? Write these lies below. After you write them, cross them out and write "LIES" over them.

4. WHAT IS THE TRUTH?

What is true about you that is represented in the second drawing? It may help to use the words you wrote next to the drawing to define the truth. Try to write it as an affirmative sentence.

5. HEAD, HEART & HANDS

Trace your new drawing in the air with your hand and arm. Say the title and feel the feeling as you do this. Picture the air around you changing to a positive atmosphere as you draw this new image in front of you.

6. REFLECTIONS & INSIGHTS

How do you feel after drawing your new power image in the air?

D3 HOMEWORK THIS WEEK

Redraw your power image for this week in the box below and write your truth statement on the lines below. Then, at least once a day this week, simply retrace your power image in the air with your arm and feel the freedom of what is true. Say the title out loud or the words association with this new image. You are training yourself to think differently. You are exchanging any current feeling of insecurity with the feelings based on what is true about you. Instead of the limiting thoughts dictating your attitude and actions, you are forging new pathways of thought that better align with your true identity and purpose. Check off your completion each day below.

1. **Redraw your power image in the box from this week's exercise and write its title.**

2. **Write the truth about yourself as an "I am" statement.**

Title

3. **Draw your power image in the air once a day this week, while repeating the truth out loud. Check it off each day.**

Day 1 ☐ I finished! Date
Day 2 ☐ I finished! Date
Day 3 ☐ I finished! Date
Day 4 ☐ I finished! Date
Day 5 ☐ I finished! Date
Day 6 ☐ I finished! Date

Optional: Take an online DISC personality test to better understand what is important to you and what your personality style is.

TRUTH
"I can live my life from love, not fear."

THE SEE JOURNEY
DISCOVERY 4
FIND YOUR PURPOSE

We may grow up thinking there is no purpose for our lives. We may have believed the lie we are random and don't matter.

UNIVERSAL TRUTH 3
EVERY PERSON HAS A PURPOSE IN LIFE

> With each human being's identity comes a purpose, which is woven throughout the desires of their heart. None can compare with another as each purpose is beautiful, complete, and an honor. Each is needed in order for all to function as a whole. Each is like a piece of a puzzle, all shaped individually, and if the shapes try to be like another, they will never function in the whole because only their shape fits their place. We each bring something to this world that no one else brings, and because of this, we are all needed and can never be replaced. Our purpose will always solve a problem, and it is this part of us that wants to make this world a better place.

With this in mind, let's consider the honey bee. It is a tiny insect, yet it fulfills an essential function in this world. Honey bees are responsible for pollinating crops that feed the world. Without them, we would lose at least 95 different crops! These include apples, mangos, plums, peaches, nectarines, pomegranates, pears, alfalfa, strawberries, onions, cashews, apricots, avocados, kidney beans, green beans, cherries, celery, coffee, walnuts, cotton, flax, macadamia nuts, lemons, buckwheat, figs, limes, chili peppers, papaya, safflower, sesame, raspberries, blackberries, cocoa, vanilla, coconut, tangerines, boysenberries, Brazil nuts, beets broccoli, cauliflower, cabbage, cranberries, tomatoes, carrots, cucumber, hazelnut, cantaloupe, watermelon, and grapes! Such an important job for such a little insect!

The honey bee probably doesn't even know how important he is. His main passion is to get the nectar out of flowering plants, so he can use it to make honey. While doing this, his fuzzy body (which is perfectly built) picks up the pollen from the flowers. Unintentionally, he carries the pollen from flower to flower, which is needed in order for the fruit to develop. Without him pollinating the flowers, there will be no fruit.

> **CORE CONCEPT 5:** YOUR PURPOSE WILL BENEFIT OTHERS
>
> Your life purpose can be found in what you are passionate about, what you are good at, and what you uniquely bring to this world. It may be linked to a struggle you have overcome that may also bring a solution to others. It will solve a problem in the world, so examining what you are passionate about gives a clue to your life's purpose.

Furthermore, a person's purpose gives them the ability to overcome any obstacles that stand in the way of them fulfilling that purpose. Do the following exercises to discover a little more about yourself and the purpose and passion you bring.

D4 EXERCISE A
THE PASSION EXERCISE

1. Is there something you have overcome in life? What breakthroughs have you had? What have you done that would inspire others to be persistent, courageous, or fearless? In what ways do you want to make a difference? If you could do anything to help others in this life, what would it be?

_____
_____
_____
_____
_____

2. Our purpose will always solve a problem. What problems in this world bother you? What injustices in this world get under your skin? What problems are you drawn to? As a child, what did you want to be when you grew up?

_____
_____
_____
_____
_____

3. What top 10 things would you want to do in your life, if you could do anything? Do not limit yourself by logic, reason, skill level, money, or location. List your top 10 things in any order.

1.
2.
3.
4.
5.
6.
7.
8.
9.
10.

4. Now prioritize these from 1 to 10 by comparing each one with another and picking the one you want to do the most. Write the new prioritized list below.

THE TOP FIVE

1.
2.
3.
4.
5.
6.
7.
8.
9.
10.

5. Evaluation your top five selections. Which ones are you currently doing? Which ones could you work on? What steps could you take today to make those more a part of your life?

Doing it!   Not yet.   If I am not doing this yet, what steps can I take today to work towards it?

☐ ☐ 1.
☐ ☐ 2.
☐ ☐ 3.
☐ ☐ 4.
☐ ☐ 5.

42 LEVEL 1 PERSONAL AWARENESS

D4 EXERCISE B
SEE PURPOSE AND MEANING

DATE: _____ SITUATION: _____

This exercise will address purpose and meaning in life. When have you felt like your life was a waste of time without a focus or passion? Allow yourself to see the situation, but hear no sound. Allow yourself to feel it and from that feeling, express it with lines in the first box below. Don't draw symbols and you may erase if you like. It's right if it feels right to you.

1. DRAW THE FEELING
Draw the feeling in the box, label it with words, and give it a title on the lines below.

TITLE _____

2. DRAW WHAT YOU *WANT* TO FEEL
*Draw what you **want** to feel in the box, label it with words, and give it a title on the lines below.*

3 WHAT ARE THE LIES?

What lies could you be believing about yourself that caused the feelings in the first drawing? Write these lies below. After you write them, cross them out and write "LIES" over them.

4 WHAT IS THE TRUTH?

What is true about you that is represented in the second drawing? It may help to use the words you wrote next to the drawing to define the truth. Try to write it as an affirmative sentence.

5 HEAD, HEART & HANDS

Trace your new drawing in the air with your hand and arm. Say the title and feel the feeling as you do this. Picture the air around you changing to a positive atmosphere as you draw this new image in front of you.

6 REFLECTIONS & INSIGHTS

How do you feel after drawing your new power image in the air?

D4 HOMEWORK THIS WEEK

Redraw your power image for this week in the box below and write your truth statement on the lines below. Then, at least once a day this week, simply retrace your power image in the air with your arm and feel the freedom of what is true. Say the title out loud or the words association with this new image. You are training yourself to think differently. You are exchanging any current feeling of insecurity with the feelings based on what is true about you. Instead of the limiting thoughts dictating your attitude and actions, you are forging new pathways of thought that better align with your true identity and purpose. Check off your completion each day below.

1. **Redraw your power image in the box from this week's exercise and write its title.**

2. **Write the truth about yourself as an "I am" statement.**

_____

_____

_____

_____

Title

3. **Draw your power image in the air once a day this week, repeating the truth out loud.**

4. **Write down your top five passions and read them every day this week.**

    1. _____
    2. _____
    3. _____
    4. _____
    5. _____

Day 1 [ ] I finished! Date _____
Day 2 [ ] I finished! Date _____
Day 3 [ ] I finished! Date _____
Day 4 [ ] I finished! Date _____
Day 5 [ ] I finished! Date _____
Day 6 [ ] I finished! Date _____

TRUTH
"I have a purpose that is unique and honorable"

THE SEE JOURNEY
DISCOVERY 5
UNWRAP YOUR GIFTS

Every person has natural gifts, talents and abilities that are designed to fulfill a purpose. This truth is seen in the fourth universal truth.

> UNIVERSAL TRUTH 4
> EVERY PERSON HAS GIFTS AND ABILITIES
>
>
>
> The fourth universal truth states that, "Every person has gifts and abilities." These talents come in a unique gift mix that is specific to each person. The truth is we all have gifts, but lies and fears will stop us from using them to their fullest potential. The lies tell us we aren't able to do it. They say we can't do anything right and that we will fail. They get us to compare ourselves to the abilities of others, and we feel that we are not as good and we never will be. These lies attack our resolve to do what we were made to do by getting us to doubt the truth that we have anything to offer.

We may have gifts and talents within, yet only see the mistakes we make. These mistakes become the evidence and proof that we don't have anything to offer. They say, "See, you are a loser. Look at everyone else. They can accomplish things, and they are successful, but you will never amount to anything." Believing these things will never encourage us to step out and use our gifts. These lies keep us in a low place emotionally; all the while, we have amazing gifts just waiting to emerge.

The lies get us to compare ourselves with others and show us how subpar we are. We compare our education (or lack thereof). We compare just about everything. Our homes, jobs, clothes, cars, and anything else that might tell us if we are a success or ever will be. We all have special talents and abilities that make us unique and able to fulfill our dreams.

> **LIES**
>
> "I can't do anything right"
>
> "I'm not as smart or talented as other people"

Wanting another person's talent only robs the world of the talents we bring.

We may need to develop our skills, which is how we build on our gifts. A person can have the natural ability for music, but the drive to practice and learn enables that person to become an accomplished musician. The aim of education should be to identify personal gifts and help build mastery in those areas that will bring satisfaction and success in life.

CORE CONCEPT 6: YOUR GIFTS ARE NOT JUST FOR YOU

People who easily give their gifts and talents to benefit others are more closely aligned with their purpose, since it will always solve a problem in this world. When a business puts the interests of their customers first, they will prosper, for this same reason. Selfishness, ego, or pride will not bring ultimate satisfaction and success, because these are based on fear, not love.

Gratitude can be applied to our gifts and abilities. We can look at the natural abilities that we have, or we can look at the things we do not do as well. By focusing on the water in our glass (the things we have), rather than the air (the things we don't have), we help ourselves stay in an empowered state of mind.

CORE CONCEPT 7: GRATITUDE EMPOWERS YOU

It is the old question, "Is the glass half full or half empty?" We can look at what we do not have, or we can look at what we have. As long as we are breathing, there is something we can be grateful for. Thankfulness has a way of pushing out negatives, as it concentrates on the positives. We focus in a new place.

There is no faster way to spiral down and lose motivation than to look at the air in our lives and lament over all those things we lack. Everyone has so many things to be grateful for and remembering these things will empower us and help us stay moving in the right direction.

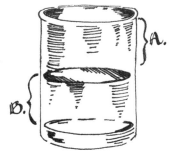

D5 EXERCISE A
WHAT ARE YOUR STRENGTHS?

DATE:

This exercise will address your gifts, abilities, and talents.

1. List ten things you like to do or you are good at.

   1.
   2.
   3.
   4.
   5.
   6.
   7.
   8.
   9.
   10.

2. What topics do you like most? Do you like sports, music, art, academics, technology, graphics, science, math, language(s), drama, choir, singing, travel, or something else?

3. Do you know how to do something that most people do not know how to do? If so, what is it?

4. Name one person that you admire for a gift or talent he or she has, and list that gift or talent.

5. What skills have you developed through education or schooling?

6. Now, after thinking about these questions and answers, list your five top gifts and talents.

MY TOP TALENTS

1.
2.
3.
4.
5.

48 LEVEL 1 PERSONAL AWARENESS

EXERCISE B
EXCHANGE INABILITY

DATE: _____ SITUATION: _____

Think of a time when you were unable to accomplish something. When did something feel bigger than you? When did you feel overwhelmed? Who was there? Who else was there? Allow yourself to see the situation, but hear no sound. Allow yourself to feel it and from that feeling, express it with lines in the first box below. Don't draw symbols and you may erase if you like. It's right if it feels right to you.

1 DRAW THE FEELING

Draw the feeling in the box, label it with words, and give it a title on the lines below.

TITLE _____

2 DRAW WHAT YOU *WANT* TO FEEL

*Draw what you **want** to feel in the box, label it with words, and give it a title on the lines below.*

3. WHAT ARE THE LIES?

What lies could you be believing about yourself that caused the feelings in the first drawing? Write these lies below. After you write them, cross them out and write "LIES" over them.

4. WHAT IS THE TRUTH?

What is true about you that is represented in the second drawing? It may help to use the words you wrote next to the drawing to define the truth. Try to write it as an affirmative sentence.

5. HEAD, HEART & HANDS

Trace your new drawing in the air with your hand and arm. Say the title and feel the feeling as you do this. Picture the air around you changing to a positive atmosphere as you draw this new image in front of you.

6. REFLECTIONS & INSIGHTS

How do you feel after drawing your new power image in the air?

D5 HOMEWORK THIS WEEK

Redraw your power image for this week in the box below and write your truth statement on the lines below. Then, at least once a day this week, simply retrace your power image in the air with your arm and feel the freedom of what is true. Say the title out loud or the words association with this new image. You are training yourself to think differently. You are exchanging any current feeling of insecurity with the feelings based on what is true about you. Instead of the limiting thoughts dictating your attitude and actions, you are forging new pathways of thought that better align with your true identity and purpose. Check off your completion each day below.

1. **Redraw your power image in the box from this week's exercise and write its title.**

2. **Write the truth about yourself as an "I am" statement.**

Title

3. **Draw your power image in the air once a day this week, repeating the truth out loud.**

4. **Write down your top five gifts and talents and read them every day this week.**

   1.
   2.
   3.
   4.
   5.

Day 1 ☐ I finished! Date
Day 2 ☐ I finished! Date
Day 3 ☐ I finished! Date
Day 4 ☐ I finished! Date
Day 5 ☐ I finished! Date
Day 6 ☐ I finished! Date

TRUTH
"I bring something unique and no one can do what i do in the way I do it."

THE SEE JOURNEY
DISCOVERY 6
BE YOUR OWN BEST FRIEND

We can be our own worst enemies sometimes. We tell ourselves we are stupid and idiots. We judge ourselves and call ourselves names, but if we hate ourselves we will find it next to impossible to love another. If we dishonor ourselves, we will dishonor others. By honoring ourselves with the truth, we will feel free to help others, without fear that we will get missed.

Sometimes, we hold grudges against ourselves and beat ourselves up daily because of it. We might think this helps us be a better person, but it rarely works that way. The resentment we hold against ourselves works against us and those we love. Science is now proving the negative effects holding a grudge can cause.

One study by Tom Farrow, Ph.D. in the UK, using MRI scanning, concluded that "forgiveness is a complex process that occurs in the brain" (Robb). He found that forgiveness and empathy "produced a distinct pattern of brain activity" and that after forgiveness therapy the brain patterns of two groups (one with Post Traumatic Stress Disorder and the other with Schizophrenia), "appeared to normalize and return to the patterns seen in the healthy control groups" (Robb).

> Forgiveness normalizes brain patterns.

Dr. Ellen Weber writes that "stress shrinks the brain and anxiety drains mental life" which causes your brain to shutdown and release the stress hormone *cortisol*. Replaying painful incidents mentally will cause sorrow or regret as the brain's "basal ganglia stores every reaction to severe disappointments" (Weber).

A team of researchers at Stanford University of California studied breast cancer patients whose cancer had spread to other areas of their bodies and they found a connection between their cortisol levels and how long they survived. If their levels were unbalanced, they "had earlier mortality" than the others (Sephton). Dr. Bernie Siegel writes in his book, *Love, Medicine and Miracles*:

> I have collected 57 extremely well documented so-called cancer miracles. A

> cancer miracle is when a person didn't die when they absolutely, positively were supposed to. At a certain particular moment in time they decided that the anger and the depression were probably not the best way to go, since they had such a little bit of time left, and so they went from that to being loving, caring, no longer angry, no longer depressed, and able to talk to the people they loved. These 57 people had the same pattern. They gave up, totally, their anger, and they gave up, totally, their depression, by specifically a decision to do so. And at that point the tumors started to shrink (Siegel, 202).

Barbara Anderson, a professor of psychology and obstetrics and gynecology at Ohio State University studied breast cancer patients and found that those with high levels of stress showed evidence of a weakened immune system and lower levels of *natural killer* cells than women with less stress. A NK cell is a special type of a white blood cell vital to the immune system. Andersen reports:

> Natural killer cells have an extremely important function with regard to cancer because they are capable of detecting and killing cancer cells. These results...suggest that psychological stress may play a role in how the immune system responds to cancer (Grabmeier).

Other studies conclude that NK cells are effective "against assaults such as viral infection and tumor development" (Vivier). Stress produces cortisol, which inhibits the immune system, producing less natural killer cells and providing less protection inside of the body against infection and disease.

A study of people with HIV demonstrated that "individuals who truly forgave someone who had hurt them in the past showed positive changes in their immune status." Other research indicates that "almost two-thirds of cancer patients identified forgiveness as a personal issue for them, and 1 in 3 of them indicated they had severe forgiveness issues" (Society of Behavioral Medicine).

> Stress releases cortisol, which inhibits the immune system.

Hostility and resentment produces stress which in turn suppresses the immune system, but that is not all. Cortisol also causes brainwaves to slow down and serotonin supplies to diminish. High levels of serotonin, sometimes called the *happy molecule*, "lead to a cheerful disposition and the ability to withstand everyday stress," while depression and mental disorders can result from chronically low serotonin levels (Coila). This explains why holding on to grudges can have a domino effect in shutting down our brains chemically and leaving our minds and bodies vulnerable to disease and depression.

Science is now proving that forgiveness benefits a person in powerful ways emotionally, mentally, and physically. Harboring resentment only hurts the one who harbors it. That is why "resentment hurts us, not them." Forgiveness may not seem intuitive and may seem difficult to do at times, but if we look at the benefits, we can be more willing to cancel the debt others owe us and live a healthier, happier life.

D6 EXERCISE
FORGIVE YOURSELF

We have all done things that we are not proud of. We must realize that all of the negative things that we have done or said were done out of fear. Fear causes torment for ourselves and everyone else. Lies eat away at self-worth, dignity, and identity. We are where we are because of what we believe about ourselves. We will never go beyond the belief of our own identity. It always comes back to identity. Changing who we believe we are is the key, but we may need to let go of regret and resentment we have about ourselves. Do this exercise to free yourself from self-condemnation and guilt.

Think of something you have done that you are ashamed of. When did you let yourself down or someone else down? When did you do unthinkable things that may have hurt others seemingly beyond repair? Hold onto that feeling. Instead of pushing it away or denying it, allow yourself to feel it fully. Allow it to travel into your pencil and come out on the paper. Draw this feeling in the first box on the following page.

54 LEVEL 1 PERSONAL AWARENESS

D6 EXERCISE
FORGIVE YOURSELF

DATE: _____ SITUATION: _____

Think of something you have done that you are ashamed of or regret. When did you let yourself down or someone else down? Hold onto that feeling. Instead of pushing it away or denying it, allow yourself to feel it fully. Allow it to travel into your pencil and come out on the paper in the first box. Don't draw symbols and you may erase if you like. It's right if it feels right to you.

1. DRAW THE FEELING

Draw the feeling in the box, label it with words, and give it a title on the lines below.

TITLE _____

2. DRAW WHAT YOU *WANT* TO FEEL

*Draw what you **want** to feel in the box, label it with words, and give it a title on the lines below.*

TITLE _____

DISCOVERY SIX 55

3 FORGIVE YOURSELF
Release any resentment you may have for yourself. Ask, "What is my wish or prayer for myself?" Draw it and label it with words and give it a title.

TITLE

4 HEAD, HEART & HANDS
Trace your new drawing in the air with your hand and arm. Say the title and feel the feeling as you do this. Picture the air around you changing to a positive atmosphere as you draw this new image in front of you.

5 WHAT ARE THE LIES?
What lies could you be believing about yourself that caused the feelings in the first drawing? Write these lies below. After you write them, cross them out and write "LIES" over them.

6 WHAT IS THE TRUTH?
What is true about you that is represented in the second drawing? It may help to use the words you wrote next to the drawing to define the truth. Try to write it as an affirmative sentence.

D6 HOMEWORK THIS WEEK

Redraw your power image for this week in the box below and write your truth statement on the lines below. Then, at least once a day this week, simply retrace your power image in the air with your arm and feel the freedom of what is true. Say the title out loud or the words association with this new image. You are training yourself to think differently. You are exchanging any current feeling of insecurity with the feelings based on what is true about you. Instead of the limiting thoughts dictating your attitude and actions, you are forging new pathways of thought that better align with your true identity and purpose. Check off your completion each day below.

1. Redraw your power image in the box from this week's exercise and write its title.

2. Write the truth about yourself as an "I am" statement.

_____

_____

_____

Title

3. Draw your power image in the air once a day this week, repeating the truth out loud.

4. Check it off each day when you have finished.

Day 1 ☐ I finished! Date _____
Day 2 ☐ I finished! Date _____
Day 3 ☐ I finished! Date _____
Day 4 ☐ I finished! Date _____
Day 5 ☐ I finished! Date _____
Day 6 ☐ I finished! Date _____

TRUTH
"I have the freedom to forgive myself."

LEVEL 2
BUILD RELATIONSHIPS

*"Darkness cannot drive out darkness; only light can do that.
Hate cannot drive out hate; only love can do that."*
— *Martin Luther King Jr.*

THE SEE JOURNEY
DISCOVERY 7
LETTING IT GO

Most of us believe we *should* forgive, but when it gets right down to it, do we really *want* to? Forgiving someone does not mean that they won't be held responsible for what they have done. It does mean that in our hearts we are able to let go of the hurt. It is not saying what they did was okay. It is saying that what they did to us can no longer effect us and cause us pain.

As we let go of the resentment toward them we are freed from the negatives they cause. We must know it is not our job to pay them back, by causing them harm, or by hating them. Thinking those things will do nothing to the other person, but it will cause us problems.

> **CORE CONCEPT 8:** RESENTMENT HURTS YOU, NOT THEM
>
> We need to understand that bitterness and resentment have negative effects on our lives and health. Forgiveness is not about changing the other person, nor is it saying what they did was okay. We choose to forgive and let go of the hurt they have caused us because by letting go of the negative feelings, we release ourselves from the pain they caused. In doing so, they no longer have access to hurt us anymore.

Logically we can make the decision to forgive and we can *will* ourselves to go through the steps. We can force ourselves to say the words and hope that it happens. Have you ever done this, only to find that every time you think about this person or incident, you wince at the thought? If you have forgiven, why do resentful feelings nag at you? Many people say you can forgive, but not forget. It may be true that we will always *remember* the hurt, but does that mean we must *feel* it. Remembering and feeling are two different things.

I have found myself feeling the hurt, even after I had "officially" forgiven. So I would find myself intentionally forgiving the same person over again whenever the same hurtful feelings resurfaced. I figured I must have missed something somewhere, so maybe a little more is needed to get the job done.

We believe that it is possible to forgive emotionally and not have to carry the negative feelings any longer. When we have completely forgiven someone, our hearts and minds are absent of resentment or hurtful feelings. Human nature will tell us to fight back, but this logic may cause us years of grief, when a better way to think is possible. Complete freedom from these feelings can be experienced. SEE offers a way to expose the feelings that have been pushed down and bring them out onto paper. They will be exposed, maybe for the first time, rather than pushed back down into the recesses of our hearts. Once we expose them, we can exchange them and be released from the hurt they cause.

This type of forgiveness may seem impossible, but empathy makes it easier. The World English Dictionary defines *empathy* as, "The power of understanding and imaginatively entering into another person's feelings." It means we take a minute to see what this person may have endured in his or her life. We know that no baby ever born wants to grow up and hurt people. That goes against the human spirit. So what negatives have they gone through?

> **CORE CONCEPT 9:** YOU CAN ONLY GIVE WHAT YOU HAVE
> Understand hurt people hurt other people and that people can only give what they have. All negatives come from fear and lies that are believed. As children, no one wants to grow up and hurt people. People learn to hurt others by people who have hurt them.

If someone has caused you pain, they are only giving you what they have to give, *pain*. Somewhere in their history they have learned it is okay to hurt others and it is from this low place that they think, live, speak and act.

Remembering that everyone is born priceless, valuable, with an identity and a purpose helps us see people in a different light. Knowing that people believe lies about themselves and live from this low place can explain all sorts of negative behavior. What would this world look like if everyone believed the universal truths?

How would we treat one another? How would we treat ourselves? If there are negatives coming out of people it is because they are believing lies and living from fear. This is a miserable place to be and it spreads misery on everyone around them. If they, just for a moment changed their perspective and believed they had value, what would that do for them? How would that change their lives? How would it impact their families?

Giving those who have hurt us a wish or a prayer that they would realize they are valuable and important is the first step of emotional forgiveness. It is showing empathy for their lives and the things they have had to go through. It is wishing or hoping that they would change and step into the person of value that they are.

> Universal truths apply to everyone, even if they don't believe them.

True forgiveness is when we can think about a person and have the ability to wish them well. We know that if they believed the universal truths about themselves, they would not be hurtful to those around them. Let's wish that all people everywhere would learn to love themselves and others.

D7 EXERCISE
FORGIVE ANOTHER

Think of someone you have ill feelings for. Allow yourself to feel the hurt feeling you have when you think of them. Picture yourself standing near them, but hear no words. Remember resentment hurts you, not them and that releasing these feelings may have a profound effect on your health and well-being. How do you feel? Allow yourself to feel it, hold onto it and draw it in the first box on the next page.

EXERCISE
FORGIVE ANOTHER

DATE: _____   SITUATION: _____

Think of someone you have ill feelings for. Allow yourself to feel the hurt you have when you think of them. Picture yourself standing near them, but hear no words. How do you feel? Allow yourself to feel it, hold onto it and draw it in the first box. Don't draw symbols and you may erase if you like. It's right if it feels right to you.

1. DRAW THE FEELING

Draw the feeling in the box, label it with words, and give it a title on the lines below.

TITLE _____

2. DRAW WHAT YOU *WANT* TO FEEL

*Draw what you **want** to feel in the box, label it with words, and give it a title on the lines below.*

TITLE _____

3 GIVE YOUR WISH

Release any resentment you may have for this person. Ask, "What is my wish or prayer for this person?" Draw it and label it with words and give it a title.

TITLE

4 HEAD, HEART & HANDS

Trace your new drawing in the air with your hand and arm. Say the title and feel the feeling as you do this. Picture the air around you changing to a positive atmosphere as you draw this new image in front of you.

5 WHAT ARE THE LIES?

What lies might that person believe about themself that caused them to hurt you? Write these lies below. After you write them, cross them out and write "LIES" over them.

6 WHAT IS THE TRUTH?

What is true about this person? It may help to use the words you wrote next to the drawing to define the truth. Try to write it as an affirmative sentence.

D7 HOMEWORK THIS WEEK

1. Make a list. Make a list of anyone you may be holding a grudge against. You may think you have already forgiven someone, so there is no need to bring it up again, but if you still have a bad feeling when you think of that person, you may want to include them on your list. List those people below.

2. Each day this week, do a SEE Exchange for one person on your list above (limit is up to six people this week). Go to the Journal Pages after the Discovery section and do one exchange for each person you still may have bad feelings for up to six people. If you have more than six, you may consider doing a SEE Exchange later for those as well.

Day 1 ☐ I finished! Date _____
Day 2 ☐ I finished! Date _____
Day 3 ☐ I finished! Date _____
Day 4 ☐ I finished! Date _____
Day 5 ☐ I finished! Date _____
Day 6 ☐ I finished! Date _____

> **TRUTH**
> "I can choose to be free from bitterness."

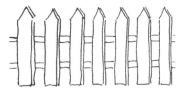

THE SEE JOURNEY
DISCOVERY 8
DRAW THE LINE

Learning to love yourself becomes the first step towards an empowered life. This becomes very important in relationships. If you hate yourself, you will find it next to impossible to love another. If you criticize yourself, you will find it easy to criticize others. How you treat others reflects how you think of and treat yourself. Loving, caring for, and honoring yourself will clear the path for loving, caring for, and honoring others.

One of our core concepts states, "People are motivated by love or fear." Therefore, negative words and actions come from fear, and positive ones come out of love. These are the driving forces behind what we do and speak. Eliminating fear helps us change how we see ourselves and how we interact with others in our relationships. Other people's off-handed comments can trigger our fears, and we can too easily take on other people's fears and garbage.

Relationships are built through honor and believing the Universal Truths about one another. When we speak truth to one another, rather than lies, we build our relationships based on what is true. Everyone is empowered in this atmosphere, but this isn't always the case. Sometimes people who believe lies about themselves like to dump their garbage on us, and up until now, we may have allowed it. If we can master the skill of not allowing the outside garbage in our space, we will save ourselves from unnecessary pain.

So, how do we do this practically? Keeping our inner life separate from our outer life is a huge key to staying empowered. We don't allow the negatives from the world to seep into our hearts.

> **CORE CONCEPT 10:** SET CLEAR BOUNDARIES OF HONOR
> One way to ensure that others are not allowed to dump their garbage in our emotional space, is to set clear boundaries with them that show honor and respect for all parties.

Set clear boundaries of honor for yourself and others. If someone knocked on your door and said, "I have some garbage I want to dump in your house," would you let them in? Would you open the door and say, "Oh yes, please come in. You can dump it on my couch." This is what happens when we do not keep the outside world separate from what is happening inside us.

This does not mean that we cannot be a shoulder to cry on and a sympathetic ear for our friends, but it does mean that we do not allow haters to infect us with their hate. Not allowing this means we set up boundaries that say what we will allow in our lives and what we will not allow.

This core concept is about being your own best friend, and it can be done without anger and hostility. It can be done matter-of-factly, stating what is acceptable and what is not. Staying empowered means we do not allow others to violate our peace, dishonor us, control, dictate, or otherwise decide for us what we are going to be subject to. We honor them and teach them to honor us by not allowing them to dishonor us or to speak to us condescendingly. We are not here so that others have a place to dump their garbage.

If you must remove yourself from a situation to maintain your set boundary, then do so. We are responsible for our emotional state, and others are responsible for theirs. Taking on other people's responsibility and garbage by allowing them a place to dump it will always leave us in a low place. Set clear boundaries that reflect honor for all involved and protect your space from others who want to cross your boundaries.

D8 EXERCISE A
BOUNDARIES OF HONOR

Set up new boundaries in your life concerning others. Write down new boundaries and what you could say or do to establish and reinforce them, if they are violated. Complete this exercise on the following page.

D8 EXERCISE B
DRAW THE LINE

Think of a time when boundaries were overstepped by you or someone else. See the situation but hear no words. Complete this exercise on the following pages.

EXERCISE A
BOUNDARIES OF HONOR

DATE:

Think about what boundaries may have been overstepped in your life by yourself or others and which new boundaries you need to set up. Write down new boundaries and what you could say or do to establish and reinforce them, if they are violated. What boundaries would help you teach others to honor you and help you honor them?

1. Who overstepped the boundary, you or someone else?

2. What boundary was overstepped?

3. Write down new boundaries that would give honor to everyone involved.

4. What you could do or say to establish and reinforce this boundary in a loving and honorable way?

68   LEVEL 2 BUILD RELATIONSHIPS

D8 EXERCISE B
DRAW THE LINE

DATE: _____   SITUATION: _____

Think of a time when boundaries were overstepped by you or someone else. Allow yourself to see the situation, but hear no sound. Allow yourself to feel it and from that feeling, express it with lines in the first box below. Don't draw symbols and you may erase if you like. It's right if it feels right to you.

1. DRAW THE FEELING
Draw the feeling in the box, label it with words, and give it a title on the lines below.

TITLE _____

2. DRAW WHAT YOU *WANT* TO FEEL
*Draw what you **want** to feel in the box, label it with words, and give it a title on the lines below.*

3. WHAT ARE THE LIES?

What lies could you be believing about yourself that caused the feelings in the first drawing? Write these lies below. After you write them, cross them out and write "LIES" over them.

4. WHAT IS THE TRUTH?

What is true about you that is represented in the second drawing? It may help to use the words you wrote next to the drawing to define the truth. Try to write it as an affirmative sentence.

5. HEAD, HEART & HANDS

Trace your new drawing in the air with your hand and arm. Say the title and feel the feeling as you do this. Picture the air around you changing to a positive atmosphere as you draw this new image in front of you.

6. REFLECTIONS & INSIGHTS

How do you feel after drawing your new power image in the air?

D8 HOMEWORK THIS WEEK

Set new boundaries. Think about what boundaries may have been overstepped in your life by others and which new boundaries you need to set up in your life concerning others. Write down new boundaries and what you could say or do to establish and reinforce them in an honorable way, if they are violated. What would help to bring honor to both you and others?

Overstepped boundary: *New boundary:*

Overstepped boundary: *New boundary:*

Overstepped boundary: *New boundary:*

☐ I finished! Date

THE SEE JOURNEY
DISCOVERY 9
CHOOSE LOVE

There are unkind, unhappy people in this world, but we must decide how we will respond to them. If we respond in the same manner and give them the same garbage they are giving us, we will become the same unkind, unhappy, person they are. We choose how we respond and what cycle we want to travel in.

We can deliberately choose love and empower ourselves every time. It takes practice to identify other people's bad behavior as fear, but it will keep us in a productive mental state and help us stay out of their garbage.

Selfish people may be difficult and we must know selfishness is rooted in fear of not having enough, so it has to take for itself. It is afraid of not being loved enough, so it must try to get love by being the center of attention. This is how fear can disguise itself. It does not always act fearful but hides behind pride, ego, and boastfulness. It is like the puffer fish that makes itself larger when it gets scared.

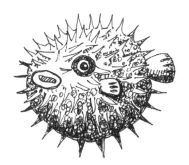

This type of fear puts others down through criticism and rude remarks. It must puff itself up because it feels threatened and it does this through conceit and egotistical behavior. It does not care if it hurts others because all it cares about is protecting itself. It is not a good place to live. The very thing that it fears (not being loved) is what it receives.

This type of behavior will not build friendships because that requires considering the feelings of another person. This fear breeds loneliness, depression, and hopelessness. Selfish people may be the hardest type of people to have compassion on. They lift themselves up so the natural inclination is to knock them down. This will immediately put us on the dishonor cycle if we find ourselves acting in the same manner that irritated us in the first place. We become them.

If love and fear are the root motivators, then every time someone shows up with garbage, it must be rooted in some kind of fear. When this happens, we have a choice to make. One option is to mirror their behavior and give it back to them, thinking this is what they deserve. They say, "You are a loser," so we say, "You are a loser!" We simply agree with their fears and lies. Whenever we agree with lies, we will disempower ourselves and others.

If we want to stay empowered we must keep ourselves on the love cycle. Do not get tricked thinking that other people's actions justify dishonor. Stay put where you are and operate with honor, truth, and love. We must become experts at seeing what is really going on and not get tricked into believing the worse about people. We need to believe the truth about them, even if they don't. It is being able to move in the opposite spirit and give them honor in the midst of their fear. When we can get to the point where we give love when others give fear, we will be able to stay empowered and productive in the most negative circumstances.

> **CORE CONCEPT 11:** MOVE IN THE OPPOSITE SPIRIT
> If people come to us with lies, fear, and dishonor, we can move opposite them. If we agree with them in any way, we will find ourselves on the same negative cycle they are on. The only way to stay on the love cycle is to give love instead of hate. This may be a challenge, but it is the only way to stay in an empowered state.

Just as a negative person can trip us onto their negative cycle, so can a positive response trip the negative person onto the positive cycle. This increases love in a person and ultimately into society. Once, we as a community realize that fear is the enemy, not people, then compassion will win over criticism and we will be able to encourage and empower each other.

D9 EXERCISE
SEEING BEYOND

This exercise is meant to give you practice seeing beyond the actions and words of difficult people. Whenever you encounter these types of people remind yourself to see beyond their fear and negativity. Think about people you are close to who have been selfish, overstepped boundaries, or have been difficult to deal with. Ask yourself, "What has happened to them that would cause this?" What are they protecting themselves from? Move yourself with empathy so you will be able to give encouragement and honor instead of insults and hate. This is the beginning of the real SEE Journey for you. This is where you successfully operate from an empowered position of compassion. From here you can avoid other people's garbage because you have eliminated your own. You can build relationships with those you care about. You are honoring yourself and others as we all process closer to the people we were meant to be. Complete this exercise on the following pages.

EXERCISE
SEEING BEYOND

DATE: _____ PERSON:: _____

Think about people you are close to, who have been selfish, overstepped boundaries, or have been difficult to deal with. Be moved with empathy and ask yourself, "What has happened to them that would cause this?" What are they protecting themselves from? Move in the opposite spirit so you will be able to give encouragement and honor instead of insults and hate.

1. What strengths does this person have? What do they do well?

2. Write down words of encouragement for this person. What could you say that would encourage, honor, or inspire? What truths could you tell him or her that might combat lies or fear that may be believed?

LEVEL 2 BUILD RELATIONSHIPS

EXERCISE A
CHOOSE LOVE

DATE: _____ SITUATION: _____

Think of someone who trips you onto a negative cycle. Picture yourself standing near them, but hear no words. How do you feel? Allow yourself to feel it, hold onto it and draw it in the first box. Don't draw symbols and you may erase if you like. It's right if it feels right to you.

1 DRAW THE FEELING

Draw the feeling in the box, label it with words, and give it a title on the lines below.

TITLE _____

2 DRAW WHAT YOU *WANT* TO FEEL

*Draw what you **want** to feel in the box, label it with words, and give it a title on the lines below.*

TITLE _____

DISCOVERY NINE   75

3 FORGIVE YOURSELF

Release any resentment you may have for this person. Ask, "What is my wish or prayer for this person?" Draw it and label it with words and give it a title.

TITLE

4 HEAD, HEART & HANDS

Trace your new drawing in the air with your hand and arm. Say the title and feel the feeling as you do this. Picture the air around you changing to a positive atmosphere as you draw this new image in front of you.

5 WHAT ARE THE LIES?

What lies might that person believe about themself that caused them to hurt you? Write these lies below. After you write them, cross them out and write "LIES" over them.

6 WHAT IS THE TRUTH?

What is true about this person? It may help to use the words you wrote next to the drawing to define the truth. Try to write it as an affirmative sentence.

D9 HOMEWORK THIS WEEK

Redraw your power image for this week in the box below and write your truth statement on the lines below. Then, at least once a day this week, simply retrace your power image in the air with your arm and feel the freedom of what is true. Say the title out loud or the words association with this new image. You are training yourself to think differently. You are exchanging any current feeling of insecurity with the feelings based on what is true about you. Instead of the limiting thoughts dictating your attitude and actions, you are forging new pathways of thought that better align with your true identity and purpose. Check off your completion each day below.

1. Redraw your power image in the box from this week's exercise and write its title.

2. Write the truth about yourself as an "I am" statement.

_____

_____

Title

3. Draw your power image in the air once a day this week, repeating the truth out loud.

4. Check it off each day when you have finished.

Day 1 ☐ I finished! Date _____
Day 2 ☐ I finished! Date _____
Day 3 ☐ I finished! Date _____
Day 4 ☐ I finished! Date _____
Day 5 ☐ I finished! Date _____
Day 6 ☐ I finished! Date _____

OPTIONAL: Do D9 Exercise B "Seeing Beyond" for others who show us with negative behaviors so you may see their value instead. Forms are following.

TRUTH

"I have the freedom to stay empowered."

EXERCISE B
SEEING BEYOND

DATE: _____   PERSON: _____

Think about another person you are close to, who has been selfish, overstepped boundaries, or has been difficult to deal with. Be moved with empathy and ask yourself, "What has happened to them that would cause this?" What are they protecting themselves from? Move in the opposite spirit so you will be able to give encouragement and honor instead of insults and hate.

1. What strengths does this person have? What do they do well?

2. Write down words of encouragement for this person. What could you say that would encourage, honor, or inspire? What truths could you tell him or her that might combat lies or fear that may be believed? Writing this does not mean you will be giving these words to the person.

EXERCISE B
SEEING BEYOND

DATE: _____   PERSON: _____

Think about another person you are close to, who has been selfish, overstepped boundaries, or has been difficult to deal with. Be moved with empathy and ask yourself, "What has happened to them that would cause this?" What are they protecting themselves from? Move in the opposite spirit so you will be able to give encouragement and honor instead of insults and hate.

1. What strengths does this person have? What do they do well?

2. Write down words of encouragement for this person. What could you say that would encourage, honor, or inspire? What truths could you tell him or her that might combat lies or fear that may be believed? Writing this does not mean you will be giving these words to the person.

LEVEL 3
STAY EMPOWERED

You were put on this earth to achieve your greatest self,

to live out your purpose, and to do it courageously.

— *Steve Maraboli*

DISCOVERY TEN   81

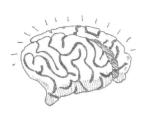

THE SEE JOURNEY
DISCOVERY 10
ENCOURAGE YOURSELF

Sometimes others will encourage us and sometimes they will not. If our motivation is determined by what others do or do not do, then we find ourselves at their mercy. We are victims and not in control of our own lives. This is why we must be our own best friend and take responsibility for our own attitudes. There are a number of ways to stay empowered: stay thankful, speak kind words to yourself, show empathy and compassion to others, use your power images, and create new power images going forward.

 Encourage yourself through thankfulness. In every situation, there is something we can be thankful for. It helps avoid the three C's: criticize, condemn, and complain. These will always disempower us and leave us in a low place. Thankfulness helps us avoid discouragement. Discovery Ten Exercise A gives you space to record things you are thankful for.

 Speak encouraging and kind words to yourself, when you feel like giving up. Why wait for others to do that job? Why give others that responsibility? It is certainly nice when it happens, but what if it doesn't? Are you to languish hoping and waiting for someone to come to your rescue? That may be a long time. Your self-talk daily can reinforce what is true about you. You exchange your limiting beliefs with the truth about your value, identity, purpose, and ability.

 Stay out of other people's garbage by showing empathy and compassion, especially if they don't deserve it. People who have been wounded in their self-worth may exhibit negative behaviors. Martin Luther King Jr. in *Strength to Love* teaches, "Darkness cannot drive out darkness; only light can do that. Hate cannot drive out hate; only love can do that" (47). Honoring others and believing the four universal truths about them is the first step towards healing. The atmosphere of honor lifts us and others to a productive, healthy, and positive way of life.

 Stay empowered by using your power images whenever you find yourself stuck or in a rut. Repeat out loud the title of each image and declare your personal identity statements for yourself, based on the truths you have learned. They help you take charge and intentionally focus your energy on a new productive image and feeling.

Create new drawings in the Drawing Journal section of this book, when you are offended, negative, or irritable, especially if you find yourself ruminating about a certain situation or person. You may need to process situations before you can move on. As you continue, you may uncover other lies you believe about yourself or others. Show compassion and empathy on yourself and on those who have hurt you. Remember, others believe lies and have fear too. Let go of all resentments you may be holding onto. Record all your exchanges, words, feelings and good wishes. Additional SEE Drawing Journals may be purchased through our website:

mkartacademy.com

To understand more fully what your drawings may be saying, refer to "The Language of the Line" section in this book. This will help you learn some common meanings to the line. As you learn this new language of the line, your understanding will increase.

D10 EXERCISE A
GRATITUDE LIST

In this exercise, you are asked to compile a list of all the things you are thankful for. It can help you to refocus yourself on those positives in your life that empower you. Complete this exercise on these pages.

D10 EXERCISE B
PUTTING IT ALL TOGETHER

Look back over your drawings and find the four that speak to your value, identity, purpose, and ability. Redraw these so that you can see them on one page.

EXERCISE A
GRATITUDE LIST

DATE:

List of all the things you are thankful for. It can help you to refocus on the positives in your life that empower you. Refer to this list often, if needed, to remind yourself of these things.

GRATITUDE LIST
I am thankful for...

EXERCISE B
PUTTING IT ALL TOGETHER

DATE:

In this exercise, please look back over your past drawings. Look for the power images that reinforce your value, identity, purpose, and ability. By putting them together, you can use them together as a group.

VALUE

In the box below, copy and draw your power image that addresses your value.

Truth

Title

IDENTITY

In the box below, copy and draw your power image from addresses your identity.

Truth

Title

PURPOSE

In the box below, copy and draw your power image that addresses your purpose in life.

Truth

Title

ABILITY

In the box below, copy and draw your power image that addresses your gifts and ability.

Truth

Title

Reflections or insights:

D10 HOMEWORK THIS WEEK

1. Referring to D10 Exercise B "Putting It All Together," write your "Life Statement" that combines your four truths into one or two sentences.

YOUR SEE JOURNEY
LIFE STATEMENT

2. Choreograph the main four drawings into a dance. Move through these images, one at a time and feel the truth each one represents. You can do this dance first thing in the morning to reinforce who you are, or before bedtime to get rid of any anxieties or fears that may gotten suck on you from the day. Enjoy yourself and allow yourself the freedom to think and move in a new and empowered way!

3. Do these combined movements once a day for one week.

Day 1 [ ] I finished! Date
Day 2 [ ] I finished! Date
Day 3 [ ] I finished! Date
Day 4 [ ] I finished! Date
Day 5 [ ] I finished! Date
Day 6 [ ] I finished! Date

TRUTH
"My identity is based upon what is true."

OPTIONAL: Read your "Gratitude List" whenever you are discouraged or feel stuck.

THE SEE JOURNEY
DRAWING JOURNAL

"If you can see it, you can become it."
— *Michelle Kamrath*

1 SEE JOURNEY
DRAWING JOURNAL

DATE: _____ SITUATION: _____

Use these pages for your own additional SEE Exchanges as challenging situations arise. You may use them for forgiveness exchanges as well.

1 DRAW THE CURRENT FEELING
Draw the current feeling in the box, label it with words, and give it a title on the lines below.

TITLE _____

2 DRAW WHAT YOU *WANT*
*Draw what you **want** to feel in the box, label it with words, and give it a title on the lines below.*
Optional Forgiveness Exercise: *If you are forgiving someone, draw the good feeling you want that person to feel. Feel it first for them and then draw it in the box.*

TITLE _____

3. WHAT ARE THE LIES?

What lies could you be believing about yourself that caused the feelings in the first drawing? Write these lies below. After you write them, cross them out and write "LIES" over them.

4. WHAT IS THE TRUTH?

What is true about you that is represented in the second drawing? It may help to use the words you wrote next to the drawing to define the truth. Try to write it as an affirmative sentence.

5. HEAD, HEART & HANDS

Trace your new drawing in the air with your hand and arm. Say the title and feel the feeling as you do this. Picture the air around you changing to a positive atmosphere as you draw this new image in front of you.

6. REFLECTIONS & INSIGHTS

How do you feel after drawing your new power image in the air?

 SEE JOURNEY
DRAWING JOURNAL

DATE: _____ SITUATION: _____

Use these pages for your own additional SEE Exchanges as challenging situations arise. You may use them for forgiveness exchanges as well.

1 DRAW THE CURRENT FEELING
Draw the current feeling in the box, label it with words, and give it a title on the lines below.

TITLE _____

2 DRAW WHAT YOU *WANT*
*Draw what you **want** to feel in the box, label it with words, and give it a title on the lines below.*
Optional Forgiveness Exercise: *If you are forgiving someone, draw the good feeling you want that person to feel. Feel it first for them and then draw it in the box.*

TITLE _____

DRAWING JOURNAL 91

3 WHAT ARE THE LIES?

What lies could you be believing about yourself that caused the feelings in the first drawing? Write these lies below. After you write them, cross them out and write "LIES" over them.

4 WHAT IS THE TRUTH?

What is true about you that is represented in the second drawing? It may help to use the words you wrote next to the drawing to define the truth. Try to write it as an affirmative sentence.

5 HEAD, HEART & HANDS

Trace your new drawing in the air with your hand and arm. Say the title and feel the feeling as you do this. Picture the air around you changing to a positive atmosphere as you draw this new image in front of you.

6 REFLECTIONS & INSIGHTS

How do you feel after drawing your new power image in the air?

3 | SEE JOURNEY
DRAWING JOURNAL

DATE: _____ SITUATION: _____

Use these pages for your own additional SEE Exchanges as challenging situations arise. You may use them for forgiveness exchanges as well.

1 | DRAW THE CURRENT FEELING

Draw the current feeling in the box, label it with words, and give it a title on the lines below.

TITLE _____

2 | DRAW WHAT YOU *WANT*

*Draw what you **want** to feel in the box, label it with words, and give it a title on the lines below.*
Optional Forgiveness Exercise: *If you are forgiving someone, draw the good feeling you want that person to feel. Feel it first for them and then draw it in the box.*

TITLE _____

DRAWING JOURNAL 93

3. WHAT ARE THE LIES?

What lies could you be believing about yourself that caused the feelings in the first drawing? Write these lies below. After you write them, cross them out and write "LIES" over them.

4. WHAT IS THE TRUTH?

What is true about you that is represented in the second drawing? It may help to use the words you wrote next to the drawing to define the truth. Try to write it as an affirmative sentence.

5. HEAD, HEART & HANDS

Trace your new drawing in the air with your hand and arm. Say the title and feel the feeling as you do this. Picture the air around you changing to a positive atmosphere as you draw this new image in front of you.

6. REFLECTIONS & INSIGHTS

How do you feel after drawing your new power image in the air?

DRAWING JOURNAL

SEE JOURNEY
DRAWING JOURNAL

DATE: _____ SITUATION: _____

Use these pages for your own additional SEE Exchanges as challenging situations arise. You may use them for forgiveness exchanges as well.

1. DRAW THE CURRENT FEELING
Draw the current feeling in the box, label it with words, and give it a title on the lines below.

TITLE _____

2. DRAW WHAT YOU *WANT*
*Draw what you **want** to feel in the box, label it with words, and give it a title on the lines below.*
Optional Forgiveness Exercise: *If you are forgiving someone, draw the good feeling you want that person to feel. Feel it first for them and then draw it in the box.*

TITLE _____

3. WHAT ARE THE LIES?

What lies could you be believing about yourself that caused the feelings in the first drawing? Write these lies below. After you write them, cross them out and write "LIES" over them.

4. WHAT IS THE TRUTH?

What is true about you that is represented in the second drawing? It may help to use the words you wrote next to the drawing to define the truth. Try to write it as an affirmative sentence.

5. HEAD, HEART & HANDS

Trace your new drawing in the air with your hand and arm. Say the title and feel the feeling as you do this. Picture the air around you changing to a positive atmosphere as you draw this new image in front of you.

6. REFLECTIONS & INSIGHTS

How do you feel after drawing your new power image in the air?

5 SEE JOURNEY
DRAWING JOURNAL

DATE: _____ SITUATION: _____

Use these pages for your own additional SEE Exchanges as challenging situations arise. You may use them for forgiveness exchanges as well.

1. DRAW THE CURRENT FEELING
Draw the current feeling in the box, label it with words, and give it a title on the lines below.

TITLE

2. DRAW WHAT YOU *WANT*
*Draw what you **want** to feel in the box, label it with words, and give it a title on the lines below.*
Optional Forgiveness Exercise: *If you are forgiving someone, draw the good feeling you want that person to feel. Feel it first for them and then draw it in the box.*

TITLE

3. WHAT ARE THE LIES?

What lies could you be believing about yourself that caused the feelings in the first drawing? Write these lies below. After you write them, cross them out and write "LIES" over them.

4. WHAT IS THE TRUTH?

What is true about you that is represented in the second drawing? It may help to use the words you wrote next to the drawing to define the truth. Try to write it as an affirmative sentence.

5. HEAD, HEART & HANDS

Trace your new drawing in the air with your hand and arm. Say the title and feel the feeling as you do this. Picture the air around you changing to a positive atmosphere as you draw this new image in front of you.

6. REFLECTIONS & INSIGHTS

How do you feel after drawing your new power image in the air?

 **SEE JOURNEY**
DRAWING JOURNAL

DATE: _____   SITUATION: _____

Use these pages for your own additional SEE Exchanges as challenging situations arise. You may use them for forgiveness exchanges as well.

1 DRAW THE CURRENT FEELING
Draw the current feeling in the box, label it with words, and give it a title on the lines below.

TITLE _____

2 DRAW WHAT YOU *WANT*
*Draw what you **want** to feel in the box, label it with words, and give it a title on the lines below.*
Optional Forgiveness Exercise: *If you are forgiving someone, draw the good feeling you want that person to feel. Feel it first for them and then draw it in the box.*

TITLE _____

3. WHAT ARE THE LIES?

What lies could you be believing about yourself that caused the feelings in the first drawing? Write these lies below. After you write them, cross them out and write "LIES" over them.

4. WHAT IS THE TRUTH?

What is true about you that is represented in the second drawing? It may help to use the words you wrote next to the drawing to define the truth. Try to write it as an affirmative sentence.

5. HEAD, HEART & HANDS

Trace your new drawing in the air with your hand and arm. Say the title and feel the feeling as you do this. Picture the air around you changing to a positive atmosphere as you draw this new image in front of you.

6. REFLECTIONS & INSIGHTS

How do you feel after drawing your new power image in the air?

 SEE JOURNEY
DRAWING JOURNAL

DATE: _____   SITUATION: _____

Use these pages for your own additional SEE Exchanges as challenging situations arise. You may use them for forgiveness exchanges as well.

1 DRAW THE CURRENT FEELING

Draw the current feeling in the box, label it with words, and give it a title on the lines below.

TITLE _____

2 DRAW WHAT YOU *WANT*

*Draw what you **want** to feel in the box, label it with words, and give it a title on the lines below.*
Optional Forgiveness Exercise: *If you are forgiving someone, draw the good feeling you want that person to feel. Feel it first for them and then draw it in the box.*

TITLE _____

DRAWING JOURNAL 101

3 WHAT ARE THE LIES?
What lies could you be believing about yourself that caused the feelings in the first drawing? Write these lies below. After you write them, cross them out and write "LIES" over them.

4 WHAT IS THE TRUTH?
What is true about you that is represented in the second drawing? It may help to use the words you wrote next to the drawing to define the truth. Try to write it as an affirmative sentence.

5 HEAD, HEART & HANDS
Trace your new drawing in the air with your hand and arm. Say the title and feel the feeling as you do this. Picture the air around you changing to a positive atmosphere as you draw this new image in front of you.

6 REFLECTIONS & INSIGHTS
How do you feel after drawing your new power image in the air?

 SEE JOURNEY
DRAWING JOURNAL

DATE: _____ SITUATION: _____

Use these pages for your own additional SEE Exchanges as challenging situations arise. You may use them for forgiveness exchanges as well.

1. DRAW THE CURRENT FEELING
Draw the current feeling in the box, label it with words, and give it a title on the lines below.

TITLE _____

2. DRAW WHAT YOU *WANT*
*Draw what you **want** to feel in the box, label it with words, and give it a title on the lines below.*
Optional Forgiveness Exercise: *If you are forgiving someone, draw the good feeling you want that person to feel. Feel it first for them and then draw it in the box.*

TITLE _____

3 WHAT ARE THE LIES?

What lies could you be believing about yourself that caused the feelings in the first drawing? Write these lies below. After you write them, cross them out and write "LIES" over them.

4 WHAT IS THE TRUTH?

What is true about you that is represented in the second drawing? It may help to use the words you wrote next to the drawing to define the truth. Try to write it as an affirmative sentence.

5 HEAD, HEART & HANDS

Trace your new drawing in the air with your hand and arm. Say the title and feel the feeling as you do this. Picture the air around you changing to a positive atmosphere as you draw this new image in front of you.

6 REFLECTIONS & INSIGHTS

How do you feel after drawing your new power image in the air?

104 DRAWING JOURNAL

9 | **SEE JOURNEY**
DRAWING JOURNAL

DATE: _____ SITUATION: _____

Use these pages for your own additional SEE Exchanges as challenging situations arise. You may use them for forgiveness exchanges as well.

1. DRAW THE CURRENT FEELING
Draw the current feeling in the box, label it with words, and give it a title on the lines below.

TITLE _____

2. DRAW WHAT YOU *WANT*
*Draw what you **want** to feel in the box, label it with words, and give it a title on the lines below.*
Optional Forgiveness Exercise: *If you are forgiving someone, draw the good feeling you want that person to feel. Feel it first for them and then draw it in the box.*

TITLE _____

3 WHAT ARE THE LIES?

What lies could you be believing about yourself that caused the feelings in the first drawing? Write these lies below. After you write them, cross them out and write "LIES" over them.

4 WHAT IS THE TRUTH?

What is true about you that is represented in the second drawing? It may help to use the words you wrote next to the drawing to define the truth. Try to write it as an affirmative sentence.

5 HEAD, HEART & HANDS

Trace your new drawing in the air with your hand and arm. Say the title and feel the feeling as you do this. Picture the air around you changing to a positive atmosphere as you draw this new image in front of you.

6 REFLECTIONS & INSIGHTS

How do you feel after drawing your new power image in the air?

106 DRAWING JOURNAL

10 SEE JOURNEY
DRAWING JOURNAL

DATE: _____ SITUATION: _____

Use these pages for your own additional SEE Exchanges as challenging situations arise. You may use them for forgiveness exchanges as well.

1 ### DRAW THE CURRENT FEELING
Draw the current feeling in the box, label it with words, and give it a title on the lines below.

TITLE _____

2 ### DRAW WHAT YOU *WANT*
*Draw what you **want** to feel in the box, label it with words, and give it a title on the lines below.*
Optional Forgiveness Exercise: *If you are forgiving someone, draw the good feeling you want that person to feel. Feel it first for them and then draw it in the box.*

TITLE _____

3. WHAT ARE THE LIES?

What lies could you be believing about yourself that caused the feelings in the first drawing? Write these lies below. After you write them, cross them out and write "LIES" over them.

4. WHAT IS THE TRUTH?

What is true about you that is represented in the second drawing? It may help to use the words you wrote next to the drawing to define the truth. Try to write it as an affirmative sentence.

5. HEAD, HEART & HANDS

Trace your new drawing in the air with your hand and arm. Say the title and feel the feeling as you do this. Picture the air around you changing to a positive atmosphere as you draw this new image in front of you.

6. REFLECTIONS & INSIGHTS

How do you feel after drawing your new power image in the air?

108 DRAWING JOURNAL

11 SEE JOURNEY
DRAWING JOURNAL

DATE: _____ SITUATION: _____

Use these pages for your own additional SEE Exchanges as challenging situations arise. You may use them for forgiveness exchanges as well.

1 DRAW THE CURRENT FEELING
Draw the current feeling in the box, label it with words, and give it a title on the lines below.

TITLE _____

2 DRAW WHAT YOU *WANT*
*Draw what you **want** to feel in the box, label it with words, and give it a title on the lines below.*
Optional Forgiveness Exercise: *If you are forgiving someone, draw the good feeling you want that person to feel. Feel it first for them and then draw it in the box.*

TITLE _____

3. WHAT ARE THE LIES?

What lies could you be believing about yourself that caused the feelings in the first drawing? Write these lies below. After you write them, cross them out and write "LIES" over them.

4. WHAT IS THE TRUTH?

What is true about you that is represented in the second drawing? It may help to use the words you wrote next to the drawing to define the truth. Try to write it as an affirmative sentence.

5. HEAD, HEART & HANDS

Trace your new drawing in the air with your hand and arm. Say the title and feel the feeling as you do this. Picture the air around you changing to a positive atmosphere as you draw this new image in front of you.

6. REFLECTIONS & INSIGHTS

How do you feel after drawing your new power image in the air?

110   DRAWING JOURNAL

 **SEE JOURNEY**
DRAWING JOURNAL

DATE: _____   SITUATION: _____

Use these pages for your own additional SEE Exchanges as challenging situations arise. You may use them for forgiveness exchanges as well.

1 DRAW THE CURRENT FEELING
Draw the current feeling in the box, label it with words, and give it a title on the lines below.

TITLE _____

2 DRAW WHAT YOU *WANT*
*Draw what you **want** to feel in the box, label it with words, and give it a title on the lines below.*
Optional Forgiveness Exercise: *If you are forgiving someone, draw the good feeling you want that person to feel. Feel it first for them and then draw it in the box.*

TITLE _____

3. WHAT ARE THE LIES?

What lies could you be believing about yourself that caused the feelings in the first drawing? Write these lies below. After you write them, cross them out and write "LIES" over them.

4. WHAT IS THE TRUTH?

What is true about you that is represented in the second drawing? It may help to use the words you wrote next to the drawing to define the truth. Try to write it as an affirmative sentence.

5. HEAD, HEART & HANDS

Trace your new drawing in the air with your hand and arm. Say the title and feel the feeling as you do this. Picture the air around you changing to a positive atmosphere as you draw this new image in front of you.

6. REFLECTIONS & INSIGHTS

How do you feel after drawing your new power image in the air?

112 DRAWING JOURNAL

 **SEE JOURNEY**
DRAWING JOURNAL

DATE: _____ SITUATION: _____

Use these pages for your own additional SEE Exchanges as challenging situations arise. You may use them for forgiveness exchanges as well.

1 DRAW THE CURRENT FEELING
Draw the current feeling in the box, label it with words, and give it a title on the lines below.

TITLE _____

2 DRAW WHAT YOU *WANT*
*Draw what you **want** to feel in the box, label it with words, and give it a title on the lines below.*
Optional Forgiveness Exercise: *If you are forgiving someone, draw the good feeling you want that person to feel. Feel it first for them and then draw it in the box.*

TITLE _____

3. WHAT ARE THE LIES?

What lies could you be believing about yourself that caused the feelings in the first drawing? Write these lies below. After you write them, cross them out and write "LIES" over them.

4. WHAT IS THE TRUTH?

What is true about you that is represented in the second drawing? It may help to use the words you wrote next to the drawing to define the truth. Try to write it as an affirmative sentence.

5. HEAD, HEART & HANDS

Trace your new drawing in the air with your hand and arm. Say the title and feel the feeling as you do this. Picture the air around you changing to a positive atmosphere as you draw this new image in front of you.

6. REFLECTIONS & INSIGHTS

How do you feel after drawing your new power image in the air?

 SEE JOURNEY
DRAWING JOURNAL

DATE: _____ SITUATION: _____

Use these pages for your own additional SEE Exchanges as challenging situations arise. You may use them for forgiveness exchanges as well.

1. DRAW THE CURRENT FEELING

Draw the current feeling in the box, label it with words, and give it a title on the lines below.

TITLE _____

2. DRAW WHAT YOU *WANT*

*Draw what you **want** to feel in the box, label it with words, and give it a title on the lines below.*
Optional Forgiveness Exercise: *If you are forgiving someone, draw the good feeling you want that person to feel. Feel it first for them and then draw it in the box.*

TITLE _____

3. WHAT ARE THE LIES?

What lies could you be believing about yourself that caused the feelings in the first drawing? Write these lies below. After you write them, cross them out and write "LIES" over them.

4. WHAT IS THE TRUTH?

What is true about you that is represented in the second drawing? It may help to use the words you wrote next to the drawing to define the truth. Try to write it as an affirmative sentence.

5. HEAD, HEART & HANDS

Trace your new drawing in the air with your hand and arm. Say the title and feel the feeling as you do this. Picture the air around you changing to a positive atmosphere as you draw this new image in front of you.

6. REFLECTIONS & INSIGHTS

How do you feel after drawing your new power image in the air?

116 DRAWING JOURNAL

15 SEE JOURNEY
DRAWING JOURNAL

DATE: _____ SITUATION: _____

Use these pages for your own additional SEE Exchanges as challenging situations arise. You may use them for forgiveness exchanges as well.

1 DRAW THE CURRENT FEELING

Draw the current feeling in the box, label it with words, and give it a title on the lines below.

TITLE _____

2 DRAW WHAT YOU *WANT*

*Draw what you **want** to feel in the box, label it with words, and give it a title on the lines below.*
Optional Forgiveness Exercise: *If you are forgiving someone, draw the good feeling you want that person to feel. Feel it first for them and then draw it in the box.*

TITLE _____

3. WHAT ARE THE LIES?

What lies could you be believing about yourself that caused the feelings in the first drawing? Write these lies below. After you write them, cross them out and write "LIES" over them.

4. WHAT IS THE TRUTH?

What is true about you that is represented in the second drawing? It may help to use the words you wrote next to the drawing to define the truth. Try to write it as an affirmative sentence.

5. HEAD, HEART & HANDS

Trace your new drawing in the air with your hand and arm. Say the title and feel the feeling as you do this. Picture the air around you changing to a positive atmosphere as you draw this new image in front of you.

6. REFLECTIONS & INSIGHTS

How do you feel after drawing your new power image in the air?

118 DRAWING JOURNAL

SEE JOURNEY
DRAWING JOURNAL

DATE: _____ SITUATION: _____

Use these pages for your own additional SEE Exchanges as challenging situations arise. You may use them for forgiveness exchanges as well.

1. DRAW THE CURRENT FEELING
Draw the current feeling in the box, label it with words, and give it a title on the lines below.

TITLE _____

2. DRAW WHAT YOU *WANT*
*Draw what you **want** to feel in the box, label it with words, and give it a title on the lines below.*
Optional Forgiveness Exercise: *If you are forgiving someone, draw the good feeling you want that person to feel. Feel it first for them and then draw it in the box.*

TITLE _____

3. WHAT ARE THE LIES?

What lies could you be believing about yourself that caused the feelings in the first drawing? Write these lies below. After you write them, cross them out and write "LIES" over them.

4. WHAT IS THE TRUTH?

What is true about you that is represented in the second drawing? It may help to use the words you wrote next to the drawing to define the truth. Try to write it as an affirmative sentence.

5. HEAD, HEART & HANDS

Trace your new drawing in the air with your hand and arm. Say the title and feel the feeling as you do this. Picture the air around you changing to a positive atmosphere as you draw this new image in front of you.

6. REFLECTIONS & INSIGHTS

How do you feel after drawing your new power image in the air?

SEE JOURNEY
DRAWING JOURNAL

DATE: _____ SITUATION: _____

Use these pages for your own additional SEE Exchanges as challenging situations arise. You may use them for forgiveness exchanges as well.

1. DRAW THE CURRENT FEELING
Draw the current feeling in the box, label it with words, and give it a title on the lines below.

TITLE _____

2. DRAW WHAT YOU *WANT*
*Draw what you **want** to feel in the box, label it with words, and give it a title on the lines below.*
Optional Forgiveness Exercise: *If you are forgiving someone, draw the good feeling you want that person to feel. Feel it first for them and then draw it in the box.*

TITLE _____

3 · WHAT ARE THE LIES?
What lies could you be believing about yourself that caused the feelings in the first drawing? Write these lies below. After you write them, cross them out and write "LIES" over them.

4 · WHAT IS THE TRUTH?
What is true about you that is represented in the second drawing? It may help to use the words you wrote next to the drawing to define the truth. Try to write it as an affirmative sentence.

5 · HEAD, HEART & HANDS
Trace your new drawing in the air with your hand and arm. Say the title and feel the feeling as you do this. Picture the air around you changing to a positive atmosphere as you draw this new image in front of you.

6 · REFLECTIONS & INSIGHTS
How do you feel after drawing your new power image in the air?

SEE JOURNEY
DRAWING JOURNAL

DATE: _____ SITUATION: _____

Use these pages for your own additional SEE Exchanges as challenging situations arise. You may use them for forgiveness exchanges as well.

1. DRAW THE CURRENT FEELING
Draw the current feeling in the box, label it with words, and give it a title on the lines below.

TITLE _____

2. DRAW WHAT YOU *WANT*
*Draw what you **want** to feel in the box, label it with words, and give it a title on the lines below.*
Optional Forgiveness Exercise: *If you are forgiving someone, draw the good feeling you want that person to feel. Feel it first for them and then draw it in the box.*

TITLE _____

3 WHAT ARE THE LIES?

What lies could you be believing about yourself that caused the feelings in the first drawing? Write these lies below. After you write them, cross them out and write "LIES" over them.

4 WHAT IS THE TRUTH?

What is true about you that is represented in the second drawing? It may help to use the words you wrote next to the drawing to define the truth. Try to write it as an affirmative sentence.

5 HEAD, HEART & HANDS

Trace your new drawing in the air with your hand and arm. Say the title and feel the feeling as you do this. Picture the air around you changing to a positive atmosphere as you draw this new image in front of you.

6 REFLECTIONS & INSIGHTS

How do you feel after drawing your new power image in the air?

SEE JOURNEY
DRAWING JOURNAL

DATE: _____ SITUATION: _____

Use these pages for your own additional SEE Exchanges as challenging situations arise. You may use them for forgiveness exchanges as well.

1. DRAW THE CURRENT FEELING
Draw the current feeling in the box, label it with words, and give it a title on the lines below.

TITLE _____

2. DRAW WHAT YOU *WANT*
*Draw what you **want** to feel in the box, label it with words, and give it a title on the lines below.*
Optional Forgiveness Exercise: *If you are forgiving someone, draw the good feeling you want that person to feel. Feel it first for them and then draw it in the box.*

TITLE _____

3️⃣ WHAT ARE THE LIES?

What lies could you be believing about yourself that caused the feelings in the first drawing? Write these lies below. After you write them, cross them out and write "LIES" over them.

4️⃣ WHAT IS THE TRUTH?

What is true about you that is represented in the second drawing? It may help to use the words you wrote next to the drawing to define the truth. Try to write it as an affirmative sentence.

5️⃣ HEAD, HEART & HANDS

Trace your new drawing in the air with your hand and arm. Say the title and feel the feeling as you do this. Picture the air around you changing to a positive atmosphere as you draw this new image in front of you.

6️⃣ REFLECTIONS & INSIGHTS

How do you feel after drawing your new power image in the air?

DATE: _____   SITUATION: _____

Use these pages for your own additional SEE Exchanges as challenging situations arise. You may use them for forgiveness exchanges as well.

1. DRAW THE CURRENT FEELING
Draw the current feeling in the box, label it with words, and give it a title on the lines below.

TITLE _____

2. DRAW WHAT YOU *WANT*
*Draw what you **want** to feel in the box, label it with words, and give it a title on the lines below.*
Optional Forgiveness Exercise: *If you are forgiving someone, draw the good feeling you want that person to feel. Feel it first for them and then draw it in the box.*

TITLE _____

DRAWING JOURNAL 127

3 WHAT ARE THE LIES?

What lies could you be believing about yourself that caused the feelings in the first drawing? Write these lies below. After you write them, cross them out and write "LIES" over them.

4 WHAT IS THE TRUTH?

What is true about you that is represented in the second drawing? It may help to use the words you wrote next to the drawing to define the truth. Try to write it as an affirmative sentence.

5 HEAD, HEART & HANDS

Trace your new drawing in the air with your hand and arm. Say the title and feel the feeling as you do this. Picture the air around you changing to a positive atmosphere as you draw this new image in front of you.

6 REFLECTIONS & INSIGHTS

How do you feel after drawing your new power image in the air?

SEE JOURNEY
DRAWING JOURNAL

DATE: _____ SITUATION: _____

Use these pages for your own additional SEE Exchanges as challenging situations arise. You may use them for forgiveness exchanges as well.

1. DRAW THE CURRENT FEELING
Draw the current feeling in the box, label it with words, and give it a title on the lines below.

TITLE _____

2. DRAW WHAT YOU *WANT*
*Draw what you **want** to feel in the box, label it with words, and give it a title on the lines below.*
Optional Forgiveness Exercise: *If you are forgiving someone, draw the good feeling you want that person to feel. Feel it first for them and then draw it in the box.*

TITLE _____

3. WHAT ARE THE LIES?

What lies could you be believing about yourself that caused the feelings in the first drawing? Write these lies below. After you write them, cross them out and write "LIES" over them.

4. WHAT IS THE TRUTH?

What is true about you that is represented in the second drawing? It may help to use the words you wrote next to the drawing to define the truth. Try to write it as an affirmative sentence.

5. HEAD, HEART & HANDS

Trace your new drawing in the air with your hand and arm. Say the title and feel the feeling as you do this. Picture the air around you changing to a positive atmosphere as you draw this new image in front of you.

6. REFLECTIONS & INSIGHTS

How do you feel after drawing your new power image in the air?

 SEE JOURNEY
DRAWING JOURNAL

DATE: _____ SITUATION: _____

Use these pages for your own additional SEE Exchanges as challenging situations arise. You may use them for forgiveness exchanges as well.

1. DRAW THE CURRENT FEELING
Draw the current feeling in the box, label it with words, and give it a title on the lines below.

TITLE _____

2. DRAW WHAT YOU *WANT*
*Draw what you **want** to feel in the box, label it with words, and give it a title on the lines below.*
Optional Forgiveness Exercise: *If you are forgiving someone, draw the good feeling you want that person to feel. Feel it first for them and then draw it in the box.*

TITLE _____

3 WHAT ARE THE LIES?

What lies could you be believing about yourself that caused the feelings in the first drawing? Write these lies below. After you write them, cross them out and write "LIES" over them.

4 WHAT IS THE TRUTH?

What is true about you that is represented in the second drawing? It may help to use the words you wrote next to the drawing to define the truth. Try to write it as an affirmative sentence.

5 HEAD, HEART & HANDS

Trace your new drawing in the air with your hand and arm. Say the title and feel the feeling as you do this. Picture the air around you changing to a positive atmosphere as you draw this new image in front of you.

6 REFLECTIONS & INSIGHTS

How do you feel after drawing your new power image in the air?

23 SEE JOURNEY
DRAWING JOURNAL

DATE: _____ SITUATION: _____

Use these pages for your own additional SEE Exchanges as challenging situations arise. You may use them for forgiveness exchanges as well.

1. DRAW THE CURRENT FEELING

Draw the current feeling in the box, label it with words, and give it a title on the lines below.

TITLE _____

2. DRAW WHAT YOU *WANT*

*Draw what you **want** to feel in the box, label it with words, and give it a title on the lines below.*
Optional Forgiveness Exercise: *If you are forgiving someone, draw the good feeling you want that person to feel. Feel it first for them and then draw it in the box.*

TITLE _____

3. WHAT ARE THE LIES?

What lies could you be believing about yourself that caused the feelings in the first drawing? Write these lies below. After you write them, cross them out and write "LIES" over them.

4. WHAT IS THE TRUTH?

What is true about you that is represented in the second drawing? It may help to use the words you wrote next to the drawing to define the truth. Try to write it as an affirmative sentence.

5. HEAD, HEART & HANDS

Trace your new drawing in the air with your hand and arm. Say the title and feel the feeling as you do this. Picture the air around you changing to a positive atmosphere as you draw this new image in front of you.

6. REFLECTIONS & INSIGHTS

How do you feel after drawing your new power image in the air?

 **SEE JOURNEY**
DRAWING JOURNAL

DATE: _____   SITUATION: _____

Use these pages for your own additional SEE Exchanges as challenging situations arise. You may use them for forgiveness exchanges as well.

1. DRAW THE CURRENT FEELING
Draw the current feeling in the box, label it with words, and give it a title on the lines below.

TITLE _____

2. DRAW WHAT YOU *WANT*
*Draw what you **want** to feel in the box, label it with words, and give it a title on the lines below.*
Optional Forgiveness Exercise: *If you are forgiving someone, draw the good feeling you want that person to feel. Feel it first for them and then draw it in the box.*

TITLE _____

3 WHAT ARE THE LIES?

What lies could you be believing about yourself that caused the feelings in the first drawing? Write these lies below. After you write them, cross them out and write "LIES" over them.

4 WHAT IS THE TRUTH?

What is true about you that is represented in the second drawing? It may help to use the words you wrote next to the drawing to define the truth. Try to write it as an affirmative sentence.

5 HEAD, HEART & HANDS

Trace your new drawing in the air with your hand and arm. Say the title and feel the feeling as you do this. Picture the air around you changing to a positive atmosphere as you draw this new image in front of you.

6 REFLECTIONS & INSIGHTS

How do you feel after drawing your new power image in the air?

 **SEE JOURNEY**
DRAWING JOURNAL

DATE: _____   SITUATION: _____

Use these pages for your own additional SEE Exchanges as challenging situations arise. You may use them for forgiveness exchanges as well.

1. DRAW THE CURRENT FEELING
Draw the current feeling in the box, label it with words, and give it a title on the lines below.

TITLE _____

2. DRAW WHAT YOU *WANT*
*Draw what you **want** to feel in the box, label it with words, and give it a title on the lines below.*
Optional Forgiveness Exercise: *If you are forgiving someone, draw the good feeling you want that person to feel. Feel it first for them and then draw it in the box.*

TITLE _____

3 WHAT ARE THE LIES?

What lies could you be believing about yourself that caused the feelings in the first drawing? Write these lies below. After you write them, cross them out and write "LIES" over them.

4 WHAT IS THE TRUTH?

What is true about you that is represented in the second drawing? It may help to use the words you wrote next to the drawing to define the truth. Try to write it as an affirmative sentence.

5 HEAD, HEART & HANDS

Trace your new drawing in the air with your hand and arm. Say the title and feel the feeling as you do this. Picture the air around you changing to a positive atmosphere as you draw this new image in front of you.

6 REFLECTIONS & INSIGHTS

How do you feel after drawing your new power image in the air?

 SEE JOURNEY
DRAWING JOURNAL

DATE: _____ SITUATION: _____

Use these pages for your own additional SEE Exchanges as challenging situations arise. You may use them for forgiveness exchanges as well.

1 DRAW THE CURRENT FEELING
Draw the current feeling in the box, label it with words, and give it a title on the lines below.

TITLE _____

2 DRAW WHAT YOU *WANT*
*Draw what you **want** to feel in the box, label it with words, and give it a title on the lines below.*
Optional Forgiveness Exercise: *If you are forgiving someone, draw the good feeling you want that person to feel. Feel it first for them and then draw it in the box.*

TITLE _____

3 WHAT ARE THE LIES?

What lies could you be believing about yourself that caused the feelings in the first drawing? Write these lies below. After you write them, cross them out and write "LIES" over them.

4 WHAT IS THE TRUTH?

What is true about you that is represented in the second drawing? It may help to use the words you wrote next to the drawing to define the truth. Try to write it as an affirmative sentence.

5 HEAD, HEART & HANDS

Trace your new drawing in the air with your hand and arm. Say the title and feel the feeling as you do this. Picture the air around you changing to a positive atmosphere as you draw this new image in front of you.

6 REFLECTIONS & INSIGHTS

How do you feel after drawing your new power image in the air?

SEE JOURNEY
DRAWING JOURNAL

DATE: _____ SITUATION: _____

Use these pages for your own additional SEE Exchanges as challenging situations arise. You may use them for forgiveness exchanges as well.

1. DRAW THE CURRENT FEELING
Draw the current feeling in the box, label it with words, and give it a title on the lines below.

TITLE _____

2. DRAW WHAT YOU *WANT*
*Draw what you **want** to feel in the box, label it with words, and give it a title on the lines below.*
Optional Forgiveness Exercise: *If you are forgiving someone, draw the good feeling you want that person to feel. Feel it first for them and then draw it in the box.*

TITLE _____

3. WHAT ARE THE LIES?

What lies could you be believing about yourself that caused the feelings in the first drawing? Write these lies below. After you write them, cross them out and write "LIES" over them.

4. WHAT IS THE TRUTH?

What is true about you that is represented in the second drawing? It may help to use the words you wrote next to the drawing to define the truth. Try to write it as an affirmative sentence.

5. HEAD, HEART & HANDS

Trace your new drawing in the air with your hand and arm. Say the title and feel the feeling as you do this. Picture the air around you changing to a positive atmosphere as you draw this new image in front of you.

6. REFLECTIONS & INSIGHTS

How do you feel after drawing your new power image in the air?

142 DRAWING JOURNAL

SEE JOURNEY
DRAWING JOURNAL

DATE: SITUATION:

Use these pages for your own additional SEE Exchanges as challenging situations arise. You may use them for forgiveness exchanges as well.

1. DRAW THE CURRENT FEELING
Draw the current feeling in the box, label it with words, and give it a title on the lines below.

TITLE

2. DRAW WHAT YOU *WANT*
*Draw what you **want** to feel in the box, label it with words, and give it a title on the lines below.*
Optional Forgiveness Exercise: *If you are forgiving someone, draw the good feeling you want that person to feel. Feel it first for them and then draw it in the box.*

TITLE

DRAWING JOURNAL   143

3 WHAT ARE THE LIES?

What lies could you be believing about yourself that caused the feelings in the first drawing? Write these lies below. After you write them, cross them out and write "LIES" over them.

_____

_____

_____

_____

_____

4 WHAT IS THE TRUTH?

What is true about you that is represented in the second drawing? It may help to use the words you wrote next to the drawing to define the truth. Try to write it as an affirmative sentence.

_____

_____

_____

_____

_____

5 HEAD, HEART & HANDS

Trace your new drawing in the air with your hand and arm. Say the title and feel the feeling as you do this. Picture the air around you changing to a positive atmosphere as you draw this new image in front of you.

6 REFLECTIONS & INSIGHTS

How do you feel after drawing your new power image in the air?

_____

_____

_____

_____

_____

_____

144   DRAWING JOURNAL

SEE JOURNEY
DRAWING JOURNAL

DATE: _____ SITUATION: _____

Use these pages for your own additional SEE Exchanges as challenging situations arise. You may use them for forgiveness exchanges as well.

1. DRAW THE CURRENT FEELING
Draw the current feeling in the box, label it with words, and give it a title on the lines below.

TITLE _____

2. DRAW WHAT YOU *WANT*
*Draw what you **want** to feel in the box, label it with words, and give it a title on the lines below.*
Optional Forgiveness Exercise: *If you are forgiving someone, draw the good feeling you want that person to feel. Feel it first for them and then draw it in the box.*

TITLE _____

DRAWING JOURNAL   145

3. WHAT ARE THE LIES?

What lies could you be believing about yourself that caused the feelings in the first drawing? Write these lies below. After you write them, cross them out and write "LIES" over them.

4. WHAT IS THE TRUTH?

What is true about you that is represented in the second drawing? It may help to use the words you wrote next to the drawing to define the truth. Try to write it as an affirmative sentence.

5. HEAD, HEART & HANDS

Trace your new drawing in the air with your hand and arm. Say the title and feel the feeling as you do this. Picture the air around you changing to a positive atmosphere as you draw this new image in front of you.

6. REFLECTIONS & INSIGHTS

How do you feel after drawing your new power image in the air?

SEE JOURNEY
DRAWING JOURNAL

DATE: _____   SITUATION: _____

Use these pages for your own additional SEE Exchanges as challenging situations arise. You may use them for forgiveness exchanges as well.

1. DRAW THE CURRENT FEELING
Draw the current feeling in the box, label it with words, and give it a title on the lines below.

TITLE _____

2. DRAW WHAT YOU *WANT*
*Draw what you **want** to feel in the box, label it with words, and give it a title on the lines below.*
Optional Forgiveness Exercise: *If you are forgiving someone, draw the good feeling you want that person to feel. Feel it first for them and then draw it in the box.*

TITLE _____

3 WHAT ARE THE LIES?

What lies could you be believing about yourself that caused the feelings in the first drawing? Write these lies below. After you write them, cross them out and write "LIES" over them.

4 WHAT IS THE TRUTH?

What is true about you that is represented in the second drawing? It may help to use the words you wrote next to the drawing to define the truth. Try to write it as an affirmative sentence.

5 HEAD, HEART & HANDS

Trace your new drawing in the air with your hand and arm. Say the title and feel the feeling as you do this. Picture the air around you changing to a positive atmosphere as you draw this new image in front of you.

6 REFLECTIONS & INSIGHTS

How do you feel after drawing your new power image in the air?

Need more drawing journal pages?

Continue Your Journey:

SEE Drawing Journal
ISBN-10: 1482606305
ISBN-13: 978-1482606300

Sold on Amazon

For more information go to:

MKArtAcademy.com

THE SEE JOURNEY
THE LANGUAGE OF THE LINE

"Drawings, like words, have meaning --often beyond the power of words to express..."
— Betty Edwards

THE SEE JOURNEY
A VISUAL LANGUAGE

In Discovery 1, you were asked to draw what emotions felt like. You may have felt lost, not knowing if you were doing it right. You may have felt that your drawings were childish and immature. If asked why you drew something a certain way, you may not even be able to say. You probably have never thought about emotions having a form or a shape until now.

I am going to show you some of the examples of drawings that Mark and I have done and I think you will be surprised how similar they may be to yours. I will explain this later, but first here are some that we did independently of each other. Mark's drawing is the first one and mine is the second. Our drawings for *anger* are very different and show two different types of anger. Mark's is sharp and is not afraid to show itself. Mine is a brooding type of anger staying in the lower half of the square frame. I definitely can tell that this is how it feels when I get angry. I boil inside not really letting it out. See other student's drawings for anger below. Are any similar to your drawing?

ANGER

ANGER

The next emotion is *love*. You can tell that the marks are much lighter and not as intense as the marks made for *anger*. Both Mark and myself drew these using circular motions and each take up a good portion of their frame. The lines are smooth, rather than sharp or hard. Below you can see what other students drew for the feeling of love.

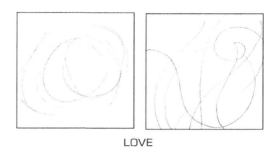
LOVE

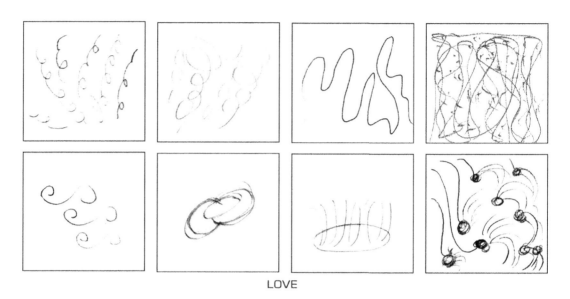
LOVE

Next, is the feeling of depression. Both of our *depression* drawings are very similar in shape and position. Notice how low they are in the frame and how little room they take up compared to the *love* drawings. All these details have meaning to our emotional minds. We can just look at these drawings and get a sense of what they are saying without even using words. As you practice drawing and reading your drawings, you will get better at both. Compare your drawing with these examples of other student's drawings. Many are dark,

DEPRESSION

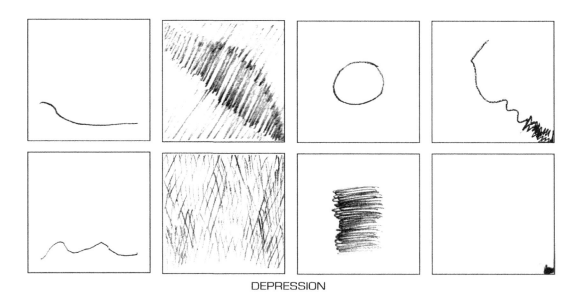
DEPRESSION

Look at the similarities for our *joy* drawings. Both start at the bottom of the frame and move up to the top. Mark's is more direct and faster than mine. You can see I took more time to draw circles at the top. It looks a bit like the lines are dancing. Both drawings are fairly centered and take up a good amount of space. Look at these student's examples below. Looping lines and lines heading upwards are common.

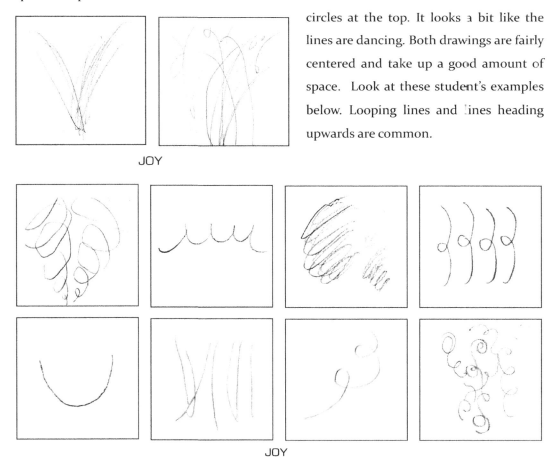
JOY

JOY

Next is *inspiration* and ours are very much alike, even though we did them independently. They both look like fireworks and are positioned in the same place in the frame. I guess I would have to say that this is what inspiration feels like to me. An idea travels up and then explodes as I become aware of it. In our drawings, we both started our lines in the left corner and then drew into the space towards the right. The action moves up from the left to the right, and there is a reason for that. Since we are English speaking and reading, we read this way and so our drawings reflect this. We did not do this intentionally, but it did come out this way.

INSPIRATION

INSPIRATION

Next, is *peace*. Again, these drawings are very similar. Mark's drawing is higher up in the frame than mine, but we both used horizontal lines flowing back and forth to give the feeling of peace. You can see feel the peace in these student's examples, as well.

PEACE

PEACE

These next examples of *confusion* are different. Mark's looks like a messy, knotted string and mine looks like someone's trail who didn't know where they were going. Both convey the feeling of uncertainty, even though they differ. My drawing starts at the bottom and wanders up towards the right corner, trying to make progress. See more examples of confusion below.

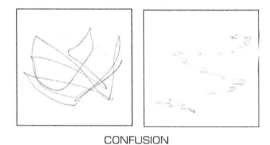

CONFUSION

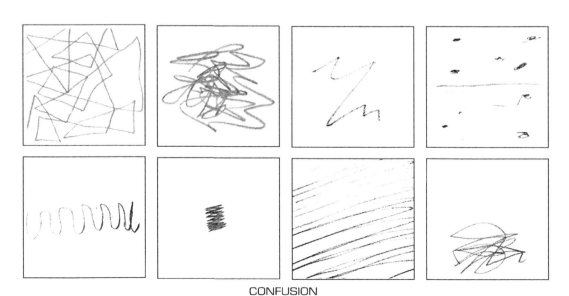

CONFUSION

Thankfulness takes on a different look for each of us. Mark's is a bowl shape in the lower center of the frame and mine looks like fans or leaves springing up toward the top of the frame. Mark has drawn this curved shape in his other drawings, so I am beginning to recognize it. He told me it represents the feeling of being held, like in a nest. It is a secure feeling for him. Mine is more of a celebration as fans or trumpets are raised in the air. See other expressions of the feeling of thankfulness below.

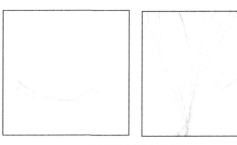

THANKFULNESS

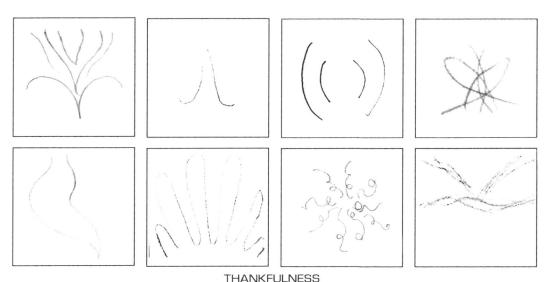

THANKFULNESS

After looking that these examples, do you see any differences or similarities to your own drawings? Our emotional drawings are based on our feelings and our connection with our world. If we feel happy, we think in terms of *up*. We stand straight and even the corners of our mouths turn up. When we feel sad, we say we are *down*. Our mouths turn down and our body slumps over. Directions and positions have feelings attached to them and these will come out in our drawings. We can begin to learn this new language of emotions by looking at them and feeling what they are saying. Being able to label these emotional drawings with words engages our rational minds in the process. We are bringing our two minds together.

ASK THESE QUESTIONS
QUICK TIPS TO READ DRAWINGS

1. Is your drawing doing or simply being? There are two basic categories for drawings. It seems either they are *doing* (linear and sequential) or they are *being* (just existing). The *doing* drawings are usually trying to accomplish something. They are moving from one place to another and you can see the passing of time and action in them. They have a goal in mind. The *being* drawings do not bother with accomplishing anything. They just exist and are not dependent on outside forces.

2. What does your drawing look like? Does it resemble something you have seen before? Does it look like a physical object?

3. What position is your drawing? Things higher up can be happier or louder. Things low can be depressed or quiet. Things in the middle can be confident. Things in the corner can feel trapped, but if the line is drawn in a corner, which one? Is it afraid to come into the frame or trapped at the other side?

4. What direction does your drawing flow? Are the lines traveling from the bottom to the top or the other direction? Reading your drawing from left to right (as reading a book), ask yourself, does the action come in from the left and move to the right? Does the left side represent the past and the right side the future?

5. What kind of line is it? Describe the intensity of the line. Is it light, soft, hard, or dark?

6. What speed is the line? Does it take its time, or is it in a hurry?

7. Are there forces in the drawing? If so, what direction are they pressing?

8. Are you in the drawing? If so, what position do you take? How much room do you occupy? Are you free to move? Is something holding you down?

9. Are others in the drawing? If so, what position do they take? How much room do they occupy? Are they free to move?

10. How does your drawing compare to your Emotional Dictionary? Compare your drawing with the patterns and lines from the Discovery 1 exercise. Are any of them similar? Could you be expressing a similar emotion as in the exercise? Your graphic vocabulary will repeat itself in your drawings as similar feelings come up.

11. What does your gut tell you it means? You drew the drawing, and even if you do not consciously know its meaning, you probably can feel what it means. Ask yourself for an explanation. Get quiet and say, "What does this mean to me?" See if things come to your mind and write all of these insights down.

COMMON CHARACTERISTICS
QUICK TIPS TO READ DRAWINGS

Linear Thought Process
The line travels across the paper as if it is going through time. The path it takes will express the emotions as they happened through a span of time. It will usually start on the left and travel to the right since this is how we read. Pay attention to the line as it travels across the paper. Does it stay level, dip down, or rise up?

Up and to the Right
This is a linear thought process and is usually goal oriented. The line may start low and to the left and then travel up and end in the top right corner. The goal is to get to that upper right corner. A sense of accomplishment may be part of the emotion felt.

Comparisons
When you compare two drawings they may contain similar elements and lines, but tell a different story. What is the same? What has changed and why?

Progression of Expression
Over time, and after drawing many drawings, similar lines and elements will reappear in the drawings. There is usually a progression in some way. Are the elements getting larger and more confident? Are feelings more able to express themselves? Does the artist feel safer and more able to express what they feel?

FORMAL ART ANALYSIS
DEEPER ANALYSIS: FORMAL PROPERTIES, SUBJECT MATTER & CONTEXT

Analyzing SEE drawings is very similar to analyzing art in general. These properties will help you see your drawings from a new perspective and may give you more insight into what they are saying. There are three divisions with which to analyze your drawings: formal properties, subject matter, and context.

1. Formal Properties

    a. **Physical Description**
        i. See the details
        ii. Describe what the lines are doing
        iii. Does it look like something you have seen before?
    b. **Contrast** (note light and dark areas)
    c. **Intensity**
        i. Dark lines are usually intense feelings and light lines are calm or happy feelings.
    d. **Quality of the Line**
        i. Are the lines curved, straight, jagged, soft, smooth, or hard? When

looking at the artist's Emotional Dictionary, what is the quality of the line for positive drawings as opposed to negative drawings?

   e. **Elements**
      i. Size of elements
         1. How large or small are the elements?
      ii. Number of elements
         1. How many elements are in the drawing?
         2. What relationship do the elements have with one another?
      iii. Position
         1. High is usually a positive feeling and low is usually a negative feeling.
         2. The upper right corner is sometimes the feeling of accomplishment, while the lower right corner can represent the feeling of failure.
         3. The center is usually confident, or being singled out and lonely.
         4. The lower left corner is usually timidity or fear to come into the space.
         5. Going outside the box usually indicates crossing a border of some kind.
      iv. Action of the elements
         1. The box can be thought of as a room that the line is interacting with.
         2. The action will usually be defined from left to right.
   f. **Time**
      i. Speed of the line. Is the line slow or fast?

2. Subject Matter

   a. **Subject**
      i. What or who is in the drawing?
      ii. Is the artist in the drawing or viewing it? Are there others in the drawing?
   b. **Perspective**
      i. What perspective does the artist have?
      ii. How does the artist perceive the feeling?
      iii. How does this perception change and what does that say?
   c. **Relationships**
      i. What relationship do the elements have to one another? Do they interact with each other? Do they touch and if so, in what way?
   d. **Theme**
      i. What is the center of interest? What is important?
      ii. If comparing two drawings, what stands out? What is different?
      iii. Two drawings may contain the same elements, but they tell a different story. What changed? Was something important no longer important?

e. **State**
    i. What is the condition of mind or feeling? What state or attitude is the artist drawing?
    ii. Is "doing" or "being" important? Is it important to accomplish something or is it important to be or feel a certain way?

f. **Sequencing**
    i. Does the line progress through time?
    ii. Does the line travel in a path as things happened to it.
    iii. Where does the line start and where does it stop?
    iv. Does it move from one place to another? If so, does it get intersected or stopped? If so, what stopped it? Does it move across from left to right making its way to the other side?
    v. Common Theme: UP and To THE Right. Upper right corner is the goal.

g. **Cause and Effect**
    i. Is one thing a result of another?
    ii. Does something precede another?

3. **Context**

    a. **Words**
        i. What words has the artist labelled the drawing?
        ii. What title did the artist give it?
        iii. How do the words add meaning to the drawing?
    b. **Narrative**
        i. What is the artist's narrative? How does this drawing fit into the artist's story and journey?
    c. **Emotional Dictionary**
        i. How do the elements in the drawing compare to the artist's visual vocabulary in the Emotional Dictionary exercise?
    d. **Symbolism**
        i. What symbolism is represented in the drawing? What do this symbols mean to the artist?
        ii. Similar symbols. A circle is common for wholeness. U for nest.
        iii. Different symbols. A circle can be negative or positive. Boxes can be negative or positive.
    e. **Emerging Patterns**
        i. Are there patterns that repeat in the body of work the artist does?
        ii. Do similar elements surface in several drawings?
    f. **Progression of Expression**
        i. Similar drawings progress over time and express more truth.
    g. **Identity**
        i. What lies are represented in the negative drawing?
        ii. What truth or identity statements are emerging in the positive drawing about the artist?

THE SEE JOURNEY
FURTHER STUDY

"Honor everyone..."
— *1 Peter 2:17*

THE SEE JOURNEY
UNIVERSAL TRUTHS

This SEE Journey has benefited people of all backgrounds and faiths. It works because its foundation is built on universal truths that apply to everyone. These truths state that everyone is priceless, has an identity, and has a purpose with gifts and abilities needed to accomplish that purpose. The belief that each person is priceless is not common in many parts of the world. Daily, people are killed, abused, and sold into human trafficking. Countries start wars that kill people for the "greater good." How much tragedy and human suffering has resulted because these truths have been trampled on?

When comparing major religions, all seem to believe these truths to one degree or another. Buddism teaches that "... all life possesses supreme dignity" (Matsuoka). Hinduism believes man is divine by nature.

> "Hinduism holds that man is divine by nature. Divinity is already within him. Our unclean minds stand in the way of perceiving it. ... Desire, greed, anger, hate, envy, pride, and selfishness are so many impurities that obscure the Divinity within man. ... As human beings we are born with the power of removing all the impurities of our minds and becoming divine in all our acts... It is then that man can see God, touch God, commune with God and even become one with God. Then really man becomes perfect" (Guyana Chronicle).

Islam teaches mankind is born pure with the ability to know right from wrong.

> "Islam teaches that human beings are born in a state of purity, as well as with a natural moral sense that enables one to differentiate between what is good and what is not. Prophets of God were sent to humanity to perfect good conduct in order to bring to fruition the seeds of virtue that reside in the original human nature. As we grow, we are able to make decisions to foster these seeds or shun them" (Muslim Student Association).

Judaism and Christianity believe man was "created in the image of God" and therefore has "inherent dignity and value."

> "While Judaism and Christianity both affirm this doctrine of the inherent value and equality of all human life, they do have different views of man. Christianity maintains that all men after Adam are inherently sinful and in need of God's enabling grace to be good. Sin, in other words, is part and parcel of the human condition...Judaism, by contrast, affirms that, humans are inherently pure and good, sin is an inclination or deed, and, humans have the ability to resist sin and initiate his own return to God Who, in turn, responds with grace" (Eckstein).

From the Christian perspective, mankind is inherently sinful, but the belief is still taught that man was originally created in the "image of God."

> "Then God said, "Let us make man in our image, after our likeness. And let them have dominion over the fish of the sea and over the birds of the heavens and over the livestock and over all the earth and over every creeping thing that creeps on the earth. So God created man in his own image, in the image of God he created him; male and female he created them." (Genesis 1:26-27, ESV)

A few chapters after Adam and Eve sinned, scripture testifies to the truth that sin did not mar the the image of God inside of man. Many scriptures support and exhibit dignity for man even in his fallen state.

> "Whoever sheds the blood of man, by man shall his blood be shed, for God made man in his own image." (Genesis 9:6, ESV)

This scripture was recorded after the fall of mankind, yet, God still honors man and woman and the value of that life. The penalty was strict for those who violated man who had the image of God inside him. The fall of man did not erase the dignity God placed on mankind and for this reason, his life was to be protected.

In Psalms, David, writes about the glory, honor, and authority given to man and woman when they were created.

> "When I look at your heavens, the work of your fingers, the moon and the stars, which you have set in place, what is man that you are mindful of him, and the son of man that you care for him? Yet you have made him a little lower than the heavenly

beings and crowned him with glory and honor. You have given him dominion over the works of your hands; you have put all things under his feet." (Psalms 8:3-6, ESV)

Centuries later, James, one of Jesus' twelve apostles, warned about cursing man, who was made in the image of God. He understood the honor and dignity that came with being made in God's image. This clearly shows that the fall of man did not invalidate the honor God bestowed upon mankind.

"With it we bless our Lord and Father, and with it we curse people who are made in the likeness of God. From the same mouth come blessing and cursing. My brothers, these things ought not to be so." (James 3:9-10, ESV)

In the book of first Peter, he writes a commandment to the first century Christians.

"Honor everyone..." (1 Peter 2:17)

This concept of mankind's value, is echoed in the redemption of man, exhibited by the Father's willingness to give His Son's precious blood for the salvation of the world.

"Forasmuch as ye know that ye were not redeemed (purchased) with corruptible things, as silver and gold, ... But with the precious blood of Christ, as of a lamb without blemish and without spot" (1 Peter 1:18-19 KJV).

God "redeemed" or "paid" for all people with the "precious" blood of Christ. The word "precious" means "costly, honored, esteemed, or beloved." The value of Christ's life and blood is not only costly, it is priceless. We know that the price someone is willing to pay for an item determines its value. This is God's estimation of mankind's value: priceless. This is true for everyone, without exception, and is the basis to the first universal truth: *everyone is priceless*.

According to the Bible, this value came from God's estimation, so nothing man does in this world will add to or subtract from that value. This value came from God's love, even while the world was in sin.

"In this the love of God was made manifest among us, that God sent his only Son into the world, so that we might live through him.
In this is love, not that we have loved God but that he loved us and sent his Son to

be the propitiation (payment) for our sins." (1 John 4:9-10 ESV)

The question remains, why did God need to pay for mankind? The first man, Adam disobeyed God's word to him and transferred the dominion of the earth God had given him over to God's enemy, Satan. This transfer was legitimate and binding. Now, Satan has dominion of the world, because he offered it to Jesus after the 40 days in the wilderness,. He revealed it was *delivered* to him.

> "And the devil, taking him up into an high mountain, shewed unto him all the kingdoms of the world in a moment of time. And the devil said unto him, All this power will I give thee, and the glory of them: for that is delivered unto me; and to whomsoever I will I give it" (Luke 4:5-6 KJV).

When Adam sinned, he transferred his dominion of the world over to Satan and legally transferred mankind over to him as well.

> "So then as through one trespass the judgment came unto all men to condemnation..." (Romans 5:18 RV).

In Adam's fall, not only did he lose his authority over the earth, but he legally transferred the rights and privileges God had given him over to Satan. Now, Satan, the ruler of darkness, was legally in charge of the earth and the people who lived on it.

God had to buy back mankind through the life of his Son. Lack of trust broke the relationship between man and God, but Jesus' trust in God and his willingness to pay the price with his blood, restored it. He gave his innocent blood as a payment for the ones trapped under the kingdom of darkness. By accepting his gift, and stepping into his kingdom, the transaction is complete and man is legally transferred back to God. He is no longer the property of Satan, but legally belongs to God. The purchase is so complete, that the enemy has no legal right to touch that man or woman again.

> "Who delivered us out of the power of darkness, and translated us into the kingdom of the Son of his love..." (Colossians 1:13, RV).

Just as Adam had the freedom to believe the lie in the garden, so do people now have the freedom to choose the truth about who God has made them to be. Anyone can accept Jesus and regain the authority and connection with God that was lost by Adam.

> "For God so loved the world, that he gave his only Son, that whoever believes in him should not perish but have eternal life. For God did not send his Son into the world to condemn the world, but in order that the world might be saved through him." (John 3:16-17, ESV)

> "Because, if you confess with your mouth that Jesus is Lord and believe in your heart that God raised him from the dead, you will be saved" (Romans 10:9 ESV).

This simple act of confession and belief transports people from darkness to the light and then into a new kingdom.

> "For our citizenship is in heaven..." (Philippians 3:20).

According to the Bible, Christians are spiritually citizens of heaven, while living on earth. They believe this new environment is the provision needed to step into the person they were made to be. They believe they were given a calling, and a divine design, that aligns with God's original intent for their lives. This is the basis to the universal truths: *everyone has a unique identity and purpose.*

> "He has made everything beautiful and appropriate in its time. He has also planted eternity [a sense of divine purpose] in the human heart [a mysterious longing which nothing under the sun can satisfy, except God]—yet man cannot find out (comprehend, grasp) what God has done (His overall plan) from the beginning to the end" (Ecclesiastes 3:11 AMP).

Christians may not know what their divine purpose is, but they still maintain they have one. They believe God formed each person and gave each one a divine purpose when each was "intricately woven" together in the womb.

> "For you formed my inward parts; you knitted me together in my mother's womb... My frame was not hidden from you, when I was being made in secret, intricately woven in the depths of the earth" (Psalms 139:13, 15 ESV).

> "Through our union with Christ we too have been claimed by God as his own inheritance. Before we were even born, he gave us our destiny; that we would fulfill

the plan of God who always accomplishes every purpose and plan in his heart" (Ephesians 1:11, TPT).

Furthermore, an individual's natural gifts and talents enable them to fulfill the purposes of their lives. This makes up the last universal truth: *everyone has gifts and talents.*

"A man's gift makes room for him and brings him before the great" (Proverbs 18:16 ESV).

In conclusion, the universal truths are found in many major religions, and especially seen in the teaching of Christ, as it pertains to a person's calling and life purpose. Being a Christian myself, I believe when God looks at us, He sees that identity He placed within us before the world began. God values everyone and has given everyone a destiny, even if they never accept it. He gives each of us an identity, a purpose, and gifts. Knowing God loves us and has given us these things empowers our lives so that we can do those things God has called us to do and become that reflection of His image that He placed inside us.

THE SEE JOURNEY
FORGIVENESS IS DIVINE

Alexander Pope is quoted as saying, "To err is human; to forgive, divine." It is this heavenly quality of the Divine that we mortals aspire to. All major religions view love and forgiveness as desirable ways to live, to one degree or another. When comparing Confucius, Islam, Judaism, Christianity, Hinduism, and Buddhism, what stands out is a difference in their willingness to give unconditional forgiveness. Confucius' central principle of forgiveness was reciprocity, giving like for like. In Donald Bishop's comparative religion's article, he quotes Confucius, "'If you recompense injury with kindness, with what then will you recompense kindness? Recompense injury with justice and kindness with kindness' and by his statement, 'Is there one word...? Reciprocity! What you do not wish yourself, do not unto others'" (Bishop). So basically, Confucius believed you should give others what they give to you and vice versa.

When considering Islam, the Quran makes room for violence if faith, property or life must be defended, and yet forgiveness is still taught in the Quran (42:37) which reads, "They avoid gross sins and vice, and when angered they forgive" (Morrison). Also, Mohammed "did not allow unlimited revenge on enemies; he insisted on kinder treatment of prisoners of war and their release at the war's end. He did not annihilate whole tribes or cities...Yet...[he] never went beyond the level of equal retribution—'...the recompense of evil is punishment like it...'" (Bishop) and the Qur'an (42:40) reads, "...the just penalty for an injustice is an equivalent retribution..." (Morrison).

Judaism, as recorded in the Old Testament, practiced forgiveness amongst themselves, but not amongst outsiders. Revenge against warring tribes was a common theme. The idea of equal retribution is seen in Exodus 21:23-25, "But if there is harm, then you shall pay life for life, eye for eye, tooth for tooth, hand for hand, foot for foot, burn for burn, wound for wound, stripe for stripe" (ESV). Modern Jews celebrate Yom Kipper, which is "a day of reconciliation, when Jews strive to make amends with people and to draw closer to God through prayer and fasting" (Pelaia). The need to ask for forgiveness is an important part of this tradition and in the Jewish religion, withholding it is discouraged.

> If the first request for forgiveness is rebuffed, one should ask for forgiveness at least two more times, at which point the person whose forgiveness is being sought should grant the request. The rabbis thought it was cruel for anyone to withhold their forgiveness for offenses that had not caused irrevocable damage (Pelaia).

Seeking and granting forgiveness is part of Yom Kipper, but the best scenario involves both parties in the process.

> Ideally a person who has caused harm, needs to sincerely apologize, then the wronged person is religiously bound to forgive. However, even without an apology, forgiveness is considered a pious act (Deot 6:9, Morrison).

This act of forgiveness is a way to draw closer to God according to Jewish tradition. Jesus taught forgiveness as a necessary part of one's own forgiveness from God, as seen in the Lord's Prayer, "...and forgive us our debts, as we also have forgiven our debtors..." (Matthew 6:12, ESV). He taught that forgiveness of a brother is a prerequisite before approaching God with our gifts.

> So if you are offering your gift at the altar and there remember that your brother has something against you, leave your gift there before the altar and go. First be reconciled to your brother, and then come and offer your gift (Matthew 5:23-24, ESV).

The unconditional forgiveness of your enemies is also a central theme to Jesus' teachings:

> But I say to you, Love your enemies and pray for those who persecute you, so that you may be sons of your Father who is in heaven. For he makes his sun rise on the evil and on the good, and sends rain on the just and on the unjust. For if you love those who love you, what reward do you have? Do not even the tax collectors do the same? And if you greet only your brothers, what more are you doing than others? Do not even the Gentiles do the same? You therefore must be perfect, as your heavenly Father is perfect (Matthew 5:44-48).

When asked by a disciple how many times he should forgive, Jesus replied, "I do not say to you seven times, but seventy times seven" (Matthew 18:22). So not only is Jesus' version of forgiveness unconditional, but it is offered for an unlimited number of times.

While dying on the cross, Jesus practiced what he preached when he prayed for those who were crucifying him by saying, "Father, forgive them, for they know not what they do" (Luke 23:34, ESV). Here were people who clearly could be labeled as enemies and yet Jesus is asking God to pardon them because they didn't know what they were doing. Giving back kindness when one is persecuted goes above and beyond the "eye for an eye" concept of the Old Testament. Forgiveness is giving the opposite. It gives love even when it is not asked for or deserved. This unlimited and unconditional love and forgiveness is said to be "perfect, as your heavenly Father is perfect" and is a foundational principle to the teaching and life of Jesus.

The ways of forgiveness for a Buddhist and a Hindu most resemble Jesus' view, as Donald H. Bishop points out in his article, "Forgiveness in Religious Thought:"

> The ethics of Jesus, Buddha, and the Hindu seers are based on the presupposition of love and forgiveness.
> ...the virtues stressed in [Hinduism] the Bhagavadgita are *Ksanti*—a forgiving spirit; *Odroha*—not to think ill of others; *Dhrti*—patience under stress; *Sattva-Samsuddhi*--purity of heart; *Akrodha*—control of anger; and *Apaisuma*—not to backbite. Pride, egoism, arrogance, selfishness, vanity, and greed are denounced as enslaving the individual while the opposite liberate.

Bishop quotes Krishna as saying:

> A man should not hate any living creature. Let him be friendly and compassionate to all...He must be forgiving, ever contented, self-controlled...

Concerning Buddha's view of forgiveness Bishop writes:

> In the Sermon on Abuse is the statement about overcoming evil with good—
> "Buddha said, If a man foolishly does me wrong, I will return to him the protection of my ungrudging love; the more evil comes from him the more good shall go with me...Let a man overcome anger by love; let him overcome evil by good...

To the Buddhist forgiveness is a way to prevent hurtful thoughts from causing harm to one's own mental well-being. This religion teaches, "The balanced person never takes offense... Compassion (karuna) is based on realizing the equality of oneself and others and also practicing the substitution of others for one self" (O'Leary). This *substitution* is *empathy* and is what Jesus showed to those who were in the process of putting him to death. In Buddhism, *mettā bhāvanā* is a meditation used to cultivate loving kindness and *mudita* meditation is used to cultivate sympathetic joy. Equanimity (upekkhā) "is one of the most sublime emotions of Buddhist practice… a mind filled with equanimity as 'abundant, exalted, immeasurable, without hostility and without ill-will'" *(*Fronsdal).

When comparing the different views on human forgiveness the most unconditional and unlimited are Christ's, the Hindu's and the Buddhist's. Jesus' example of forgiveness is grounded in God's good will toward mankind and His unconditional provision seen in nature, when he taught "…For he makes his sun rise on the evil and on the good… You therefore must be perfect, as your heavenly Father is perfect." The quality of this kind of forgiveness originates in the Divine and breathes freedom into those who aspire to live at its level.

WORKS CITED

Bishop, Donald H., "Forgiveness in Religious Thought". Studies in Comparative Religion <http://www.studiesincomparativereligion.com/public/articles/Forgiveness_in_Religious_Thought-by_Donald_H_Bishop.aspx> 2007. (accessed 21 August 2013).

Borchard, T. (2010). The Power of Forgiveness. Psych Central. from <http://psychcentral com/blog/archives/2010/05/21/the-power-of-forgiveness/> (accessed 8 June 2013).

Collins English Dictionary – Complete and Unabridged © HarperCollins Publishers 1991, 1994, 1998, 2000, 2003

Coila, Bridget. "Effects of Serotonin on the Body" Live Strong Foundation. 20 June 2010. <http://www.livestrong.com/article/154361-effects-of-serotonin-on-the-body/#ixzz2cYEgPhVB>

Eckstein, Rabbi Yechiel. "Jewish Concepts: Judaism On The Worth Of Every Person." Jewish Virtual Library. 2022 https://www.jewishvirtuallibrary.org/judaism-on-the-worth-of-every-person (accessed 28 April 2022).

Fronsdal, Gil. "Equanimity." Insight Meditation Center. <http://www.insightmeditationcenter.org/books-articles/articles/equanimity/> 29 May 2004. (accessed 22 August 2013).

Grabmeier, Jeff. "Study Finds Link Between Stress, Immune System in Cancer Patients." <http://researchnews.osu.edu/archive/apastre1.htm> 10 February 1995. (accessed 17 August 2013).

Guyana Chronicle. "The importance of man in Hinduism." 24 June 2010.<https://guyanachronicle.com/2010/06/24/the-importance-of-man-in-hinduism/#:~:text=Editor%2C%20in%20our%20Hindu%20language,is%20 blessed%20with%20divine%20intelligence.> (accessed 28 April 2022).

Luskin, Frederic. Forgive For Good: A Proven Prescription for Health and Happiness. San Francisco: Harper, 2002.

Mandela, Nelson Rolihlahla. *Long Walk to Freedom*. New York: Little, Brown and Company, 1995.

Matsuoka, Mikio. "The Buddhist Concept of the Human Being: From the Viewpoint of the Philosophy of the Soka Gakkai" <https://www.totetu.org/assets/media/paper/jo15_050.pdf> (accessed 29 April 2022) page 57.

Muslim Student Association. "What Does the Quran Say About Humanity?" <https://sites.ualberta.ca/~msa/pdf/quran_humanity.pdf> (accessed 28 April 2022).

Morrison, Deborah. "Forgiveness in Different Religions". Nexus. 2007. <http://nexusnovel.wordpress.com/2007/01/03/forgiveness-in-different-religions/> (accessed 21 August 2013).

O'Leary, Joseph S., "Buddhism and Forgiveness." ZBOHY. <http://www.hsuyun.org/index.php/features1/outreach/607-forgiveness.html> First published in Dharma World 31, Nov.-Dec. 2004 (accessed 22 August 2013).

Pelaia, Ariela. "What Is Yom Kippur?" Judaism About.com <http://judaism.about.com/od/holidays/a/yomkippur.htm> 15 July 2013. (accessed 21 August 2013).

Robb, Vicki. "First Study to Watch Brain Patterns When Forgiving." EurekAlert.org. <http://www.eurekalert.org/pub_releases/2003-10/cff-fst100803.php> 8 October 2003 (accessed 23 August 2013).

Sephton, S.E., Sapolsky, R.M, Kraemer, H.C., and Spiegel, D., Diurnal Cortisol Rhythm as a Predictor of Breast Cancer Survival. JNCI Journal of the National Cancer Institution. <http://jnci.oxfordjournals.org/content/92/12/994.full> (accessed 20 August 2013).

Siegel, Bernie S. *Love, Medicine and Miracles*, William Morrow Paperbacks; Reissue edition (July 22, 1998).

Society of Behavioral Medicine (SBM) 32nd Annual Meeting and Scientific Sessions: Abstract 4010. Presented April 30, 2011.

Tipping, Colin. Radical Forgiveness: A Revolutionary Five-Stage Process to Heal Relationships, Let Go of Anger and Blame, Find Peace in Any Situation, Sounds True, Incorporated; Un abridged edition (December 28, 2009).

Vivier, E., Raulet, D.H., Moretta, A., Caligiuri, M.A., Zitvogel, L., Lanier, L.L., Yokoyama, W.M. & Ugolini, S. (2011). "Innate or Adaptive Immunity? The Example of Natural Killer Cells". Science 331: 44–49. <http://www.sciencemag.org/content/331/6013/44>. (accessed 20 August 2013).

Weber, Ellen. "A Brain on Forgiveness." Brain Leaders and Learners. 17 September 2011 <http://www.brainleadersandlearners.com/amygdala/a-brain-on-forgiveness> (accessed 10 August 2013).

Worthington, Everett, Jr. A Campaign for Forgiveness Research. 2005. <http://www.forgiving.org> (accessed 10 June 2013).

OTHER PUBLICATIONS
BY MICHELLE KAMRATH

Sold on Amazon

SEE Drawing Journal
This journal gives you 50 blank formatted SEE Journey pages so you can continue drawing after you complete The SEE Journey courses or books. The SEE process empowers the whole person by connecting the creative and rational minds. — 132 pages.
ISBN-10 1482606305 Available on Amazon

Emerging Art: Student Edition
Emerging Art Student Edition is an instructional art textbook intended for grades 7-12. It covers the Elements of Art and the Principles of Design through twelve chapters with 108 step-by-step exercises. Includes 56 creativity tips and 12 creative thinking activities. Addresses and notes the National Core Art Standards throughout the book. Studies 12 famous artists and teaches formal art appreciation. — 200 pages full color.
ISBN-10 1733036806   Available on Amazon

Emerging Art: Teacher Edition
This book is a reproduction of the full color 200 page *Emerging Art: Student Edition* with an added Teacher Section of 114 pages, which includes 86 chapter worksheets, review answers, 13 tests, test answers and evaluation forms. — 314 pages full color.
ISBN-10 1733036814   Available on Amazon

For more information go to:

mkartacademy.com

Made in the USA
Middletown, DE
11 May 2022